The Days are Numbered: Book 1

DAYSTAR

www.kayleenwest.com.au

ANNE HAMILTON
Teacher's Resource

Daystar: The Days are Numbered Book 1
Teaching Resource
Published by Wombat Books, 2016
PO Box 1519, Capalaba Qld 4157
www.wombatbooks.com.au

Cover Illustration by Carmen Dougherty
Inside Cover Illustration by Kayleen West
Decorative Initials by Rose SK
Design and activities by Anne Hamilton

© Anne Hamilton 2016

ISBN: 978-1-925139-74-7

National Library of Australia Cataloguing-in-Publication entry available

All rights reserved. No part of this publication may be reproduced, stored in, or introduced into a retrieval system, or transmitted, in any form, or by any means (electronic, mechanical, photocopying, recording or otherwise) without the prior written permission of the publisher.

Special thanks to:
Lisa and Eva

These notes and blackline masters may be reproduced free of charge, provided they are used solely for the purpose of studying the novel *The Days are Numbered Book 1: Daystar* within schools as part of the classroom curriculum. They may not be reproduced, either in whole or in part, in any format for commercial sale or re-sale.

Teacher's Notes 1:

The following index of names is reproduced for your convenience from *The Days are Numbered Book 1: Daystar*. Students may consult the index in the novel.

INDEX OF NAMES

Ancient of Days

The High King, the Timeless One, The Lord of Days

Anomalous Duality

An object in two places at once

Ansey

Nickname for the crown prince and heir to the kingdom of Auberon; one of the Seven Days; Sunday's Child

Ancelin Bedwyr Cai

See Ansey

Ancelin, Lord of Tariquhaven

Former best friend to the king of Auberon; Ansey is his namesake

Apprentice in Intrigue

A position Candle wants to give Dallan

Ashe, Mrs (Miz)

A chaplain at Fern's school; the registrar for race entrants on school sports day

Auberon

A kingdom ruled by king Maurtz; one of the seven kingdoms carved out of the ancient principality of Auberon–Zamberg

Auberon–Zamberg

An ancient principality, later divided into seven Kingdoms, six of which are known and one of which is hidden

Barbizca

The second wife of Maurtz, king of Auberon

Battle of Tariquhaven

Battle in which Ancelin was given the title 'Lord of Tariquhaven' for killing two giant brothers and saving the life of King Maurtz

Belt of Veracity

One of the Seven Powers; in the care of the dwarves of the Nardelf; Candle wears it

Boody

Nickname of a baby white owl; one of the Seven Days; Thursday's Child

Boudicca's Chariot

See Boody

Bowl of the Field of Stars

Also called 'Basin of the Field of Stars'; a cirque carved out by a glacier in which time eddies are frequent occurrences

Boy Wonder

A slightly sarcastic nickname used by Hector for Dallan

Bramble

A dwarf who watched the flight of the tutors from Fastness Height

Callum

A march-lord with responsibility for keeping watch on the border forts of Auberon

Candle

A dwarf; the anointed High King of the Cavern Kin, also titled Lord of The Nardelf, Enthroned Serenity on the Rock of Time, Master of The Deeping Ways, Warden of the Scimitar Mountains, Well-builder of the Stars, Son of Earth and Child of Ancient Dream

Cato

An injured runner

Cavern Kin

Dwarves

Cindurrah

See Madmerry; means *star-shepherd*

City of Mages

A place visited by Uller in search of the scroll about *The King Who Guards the Gate*

Companion to the Heir of Auberon

See Candle

Dallan

A blind and autistic sheep-herder; a friend of Madmerry

Danika

Hector's mother

Dark Dragon

See Dark Sleeper

Dark Flyer

See Dark Sleeper

Dark Sleeper

A malevolent entity which is waking but, while in sleep, constantly tugs at a 'blanket' formed by the surface of the land.

Dark Walker

See Dark Sleeper

Daystar

A title of the Ancient of Days

Daystar Shield

One of the Seven Powers; it cannot be awakened except by a kiss from the Ancient of Days

Doctor Much

One of Ansey's tutors

Eagle Legion

A troop of dwarves watching the Bowl of the Field of Stars

Ector

See Hector

Efreets

Ally of the Jotuns

Elsa

Fern's step-sister

Emyr

Prince of Fyrzentsou; he can be identified by his one green eye and one blue eye

Fateweaver

A weaver with the ability to twine the fates of individuals using a special shuttle

Fern McDey

A girl who finds security in being 'invisible'; one of the Seven Days (although originally a substitute); Monday's Child

Fifth Dwarf Legion

Dwarf troop that appears on the rim of the Bowl of the Field of Stars

Flair

An instinctive ability to understand the language of a different species; the two main varieties are Beast Flair and Bird Flair; a sign of the bloodline covenant over the rulers of Auberon

Fletch

A strategy board game, combining skill and strange chance

Flower of Heart's Desire

A gift given to Emyr by Candle; a crafted living daisy

Freutim

King of the frost giants, ruler of the Jotun alliance

Fyrzentsou

A kingdom ruled by the usurper Rogin; one of the seven kingdoms carved out of the ancient principality of Auberon-Zamberg

Ginevra

A white baby fawn; one of the Seven Days; Wednesday's Child

Ginevra-'ayelet-hashachar

The full name of the white baby fawn, Ginevra; one of the Seven Days; Wednesday's Child. 'ayelet-hashachar is Hebrew for 'gazelle of dawn', a name of the morning star.

Goliath Jones

A fast midget who fights anyone who calls him 'Golly'; he has an eye for Elsa

Grace Cloaks

Rainbow-coloured mantles with different gifts to bestow; each hums a musical note

Gratian

The new captain of the King's Shield; the commander of Ysgarde

Harper

One of Ansey's tutors

Harrowfell

A steep cliff-face with a dangerous switchback road running up it

Hector

A white baby fox; one of the Seven Days; Tuesday's Child

Helmet of Providence

One of the Seven Powers; in the care of the Kingdom of Fyrzentsou; disguised by an over-mask; also called 'The Helmet of Time'

His Q-ness

See Quystein

Hobbit

A nickname of Goliath Jones

Huginn

One of Uller Princekiller's ravens

Humble

A dwarf sent to Fyrzentsou to help Gratian and the tutors

Imri

The murdered king of Fyrzentsou; nicknamed 'The Whirlwind'; father of Emyr and husband of Olethea

Isles of the Colossus

A place visited by Uller in search of *The King Who Guards the Gate*

Jens

A boy who once lent Ansey his practice sword

Jénève

The first wife of Maurtz, king of Fyrzentsou

Jotuns

Giants; Jotuns could be frost giants, storm giants or fire giants

Khufu

Pharoah of ancient Egypt; builder of a pyramid

Kindle

A dwarf sent to Fyrzentsou to help Gratian and the tutors

Kingdoms Beneath the Sea

A place visited by Uller in search of *The King Who Guards the Gate*

King Who Guards the Gate

A scroll of prophecy about the end of the age referring to king set to guard a gate against giants and also referring to the coming of the Daystar

King's Shield

A troop of soldiers specifically assigned to protect King Maurtz and Castle Auberon

Knights of Renown

An independent band of knights from Ysgarde, famed for their integrity which is shown by the brightness of their shields

Lal

One of the servants at Ysgarde; also called Lally

Lance

See Ancelin, Lord of Fatehaven

Land-bond

A spiritual bond between the rulers of Fyrzentsou and their land for the health of the land; a sign of the bloodline covenant over the rulers of Fyrzentsou

Lyndark

A distant kingdom; one of the seven kingdoms carved out of the ancient principality of Auberon-Zamberg

Madder's Crossing

A river crossing with an old decaying bridge

Madmerry

A girl whose face is so scarred she wears a fantastic mask to hide it; a herbalist; one of the Seven Days; Friday's Child

Mailcoat of Justice

One of the Seven Powers; in the care of the Sovereign Isles; stolen by the Jotuns; looks like a silver collar

Malveraine

A distant kingdom; one of the seven kingdoms carved out of the ancient principality of Auberon-Zamberg

Manticores

A rust-coloured human-faced lion with the tail of a scorpion and green blood

Mara-mares

Embodied spirits of nightmares

Merry

See Madmerry

Messenger Shoes

One of the Seven Powers; in the care of the Kingdom of Malveraine; lost and found by a den of foxes

Mintaka

Captain Gratian's horse; it is the name of a star in the constellation Orion.

Mistmurk

A vast swamp

Mistmurk Height

A high ridge jutting into and overlooking the Mistmurk swamp

Mistress of Illusion

A title used for female Jotuns who can skinchange or shapechange (that is, disguise their appearance by a 'second skin')

Mistress Wildling

A title Candle used to address Madmerry

Mouse

A nickname of Goliath Jones

Munin

One of Uller Princekiller's ravens

Nardelf

An underground kingdom ruled by Candle; the realm of the dwarves; the hidden one of the seven kingdoms carved out of the ancient principality of Auberon-Zamberg

Nero

Emperor of Rome; owner of a vomitorium

Nick

Fern's step-father

Nine Netherhells

A reference in a curse by Gratian

Nobble

A dwarf who escorted the Days to Ysgarde

Old Greywhiskers

One of Ansey's tutors

Olethea

Emyr's mother; former queen of Fyrzentsou

Olien

Emyr's aunt; queen of Fyrzentsou

Osiirians

An ancient race, long disappeared; green-hued

Parment

Patricus Percival Parment; usual gatekeeper at Ysgarde

Professor

See Old Greywhiskers

Puddle

A dwarf, a Subtle Gentle, an artist whose greatest work of art was her own life

Quade

A boy Fern was asked to befriend.

Quystein

Acting commander of the Knights of Renown

Rhodri Harke

A cowardly knight

Rigel

A horse ridden by Ansey and calmed using the Flair; it is the name of a star in the constellation Orion.

Rogin

King of Fyrzentsou; a usurper

Rubble

A dwarf who watched the flight of the tutors from Fastness Height

Ruēl

Name of the Creator, see Ancient of Days

Seven Days

The seven chosen ones of prophecy; unexpectedly discovered to be children; not all of them are human

Seven Powers

Six are known, one is hidden; the Seven Days need to use the Seven Powers to defeat the Dark Sleeper

Snow Citadel of the Wreathwatch Wraiths

Solveigra's castle in the Wreathwatch Mountains; abode of snow demons

Solveigra

An ancient queen who wished for immortality; her legend is told more fully in **Many-Coloured Realm**

Sovereign Isles

A distant kingdom; one of the seven kingdoms carved out of the ancient principality of Auberon-Zamberg

Speaking Sword

One of the Seven Powers; in the care of the Kingdom of Vircontium; stolen by the frost giants

Squeak

A nickname of Goliath Jones

Subtle Gentles

Dwarf artists whose works of art are their own lives

Summerheight

Middle of the season of summer

The Q

See Quystein

The Song

See Ancient of Days

Tobias

One of Ansey's tutors

Toddle

A dwarf sent to Fyrzentsou to help Gratian and the tutors

Trolls

Allies of the Jotuns

Tybold

Ansey's step-brother; son of Barbizca

Uller Princekiller

A frost giant who has sought for the identity of The King Who Guards the Gate for many centuries

Van

One of the servants at Ysgarde

Vircontium

A distant kingdom famous for its swordmasters; one of the seven kingdoms carved out of the ancient principality of Auberon–Zamberg

White Mother

See Solveigra

Winterdeep

Middle of the season of winter

Wobble

A dwarf who escorted the Days to Ysgarde

Wreathwatch Mountains

A range of mountain peaks forming part of the border between Auberon and Fyrzentsou

Wreathwatch Pass

A mountain pass between Auberon and Fyrzentsou; part of it glaciated; guarded by the White Mother

Wreathwatch Woman

See Solveigra

Xerxes Xenophon

Human resource manager and slave trader; disguise of Uller Princekiller

Ysanne

A knight at Ysgarde

Zippy

A pony

WonderWord 1

Chapter A[1] ~ Level: *easy*

Directions for words are ⇨ ⇦ ⇧ ⇩

R	H	P	I	H	W	A
U	O	O	H	C	E	N
N	R	M	I	S	T	C
Y	S	G	A	R	D	E
Z	E	R	I	G	E	L
F	U	R	R	O	W	I
G	R	A	T	I	A	N

Find the following words:

- Ancelin
- Gratian
- Ysgarde
- Rigel
- horse
- mist
- whip
- furrow
- echo
- run

There is one left-over letter. What is it? ....

Wordcloud

This is a wordcloud for Chapter 1 of *Daystar*. Using some of your own writing, create your own wordcloud on the net at *Wordle*. Wordle removes common words like 'the', 'and' (and the like) and sizes the words according to how often they appear.

Teachers please note: Javascript plugin is needed to access the Wordle site. If this is disabled, students may not be able to complete this exercise. Please note the FAQs at Wordle regarding displays of inappropriate wordclouds on the site.

WonderWord 2

Chapter A[1] ~ Level: *easy*

Directions for words are ⇒ ⇐ ⇑ ⇓

A	N	C	E	L	I	N
S	T	A	S	P	F	A
E	H	P	C	M	O	I
S	I	T	A	A	L	T
R	E	A	P	W	D	A
O	F	I	E	S	S	R
H	A	N	R	O	H	G

Find the following words:

- Ancelin
- Gratian
- captain
- thief
- horses
- horn
- folds
- escape
- swamp

Vocabulary in Chapter A[1]

1. **agitation** — a state of shaken emotions
2. **arrogant** — overbearing or insolently proud
3. **charger** — a horse suitable for riding in battle
4. **contort** — twist, bend or draw out of shape
5. **converge** — head towards a common meeting point
6. **ferment** — to be agitated or troubled
7. **flail** — swing freely
8. **furrow** — a groove in the ground
9. **pommel** — the part that sticks out at the top of a saddle
10. **ruse** — a trick
11. **smirk** — smile in an offensive way
12. **tortuous** — full of twists, turns or bends
13. **whicker** — neigh or whinny of a horse

Research what a saddle and pommel look like, then draw both saddle and pommel on the horse at right.

CLOZE ~ 1

Ansey hears the ringing echo of a _____ and pats the horse named _____. Only when he sees cloud shadow in the shape of wolf _____ flying against the _____ does he realise he's been tricked.

He is captured on the edge of a marsh called the _____. The soldiers who catch him discover that he was able to tame the savage horse because he has a gift called _____.

They take him across the countryside which shows wrinkling and _____. The soldiers think that dark _____ has cursed the land and that it's not as _____ from one place to another as it used to be. Ansey tries to escape when an _____ occurs but does _____ succeed.

Choosing **Names** 1

The names of the characters in *Daystar* are very carefully chosen. In ancient times, naming was a sacred trust. Sometimes children did not receive their names for a long time. They might have had to wait until they were baptised at church or had gone through a ceremony of dedication or until the tribal elders had observed them for long enough to know what their name should be so that it would reflect both their identity and their destiny.

If you were to **receive a name for the first time** today, **what meaning would suit you**?

If you were named after an animal, would Tiger or Panda be more appropriate? If you were named after a bird, would it be Sparrow or Hawk or even Sparrowhawk? If you were named after a plant, would it be Rose or Dandelion or Thorn? If you were named after a colour, would you be Scarlet or Cobalt or Xanthe?

Divide up the following tasks amongst the members of your group.

- Research animal names in your group. List them on the back. Try to find at least one for each letter of the alphabet.
- Research bird names in your group. List them on the back. Try to find at least one for each letter of the alphabet.
- Research plant or flower names in your group. List them on the back. Try to find at least one for each letter of the alphabet.
- Research colour names in your group. List them on the back. Try to find at least one for each letter of the alphabet. (And yes, there is one for X!)

Now that you have the information, share it with your group. Now answer the following:

An animal name I think suits me:

An animal name the group thinks suits me:

A bird name I think suits me:

A bird name the group thinks suits me:

A plant or flower name I think suits me:

A plant name the group thinks suits me:

A colour name I think suits me:

A colour name the group thinks suits me:

Choose two from the list to make a new name, eg. Lilac Yak or Moss Falcon:

My real name:

A new name that suits me:

Animal Names	Bird Names	Plant Names	Colour Names
A	A	A	A ....
B	B	B	B ....
C	C	C	C ....
D	D	D	D ....
E	E	E	E ....
F	F	F	F ....
G	G	G	G ....
H	H	H	H ....
I	I	I	I ....
J	J	J	J ....
K	K	K	K ....
L	L	L	L ....
M	M	M	M ....
N	N	N	N ....
O	O	O	O ....
P	P	P	P ....
Q	Q	Q	Q ....
R	R	R	R ....
S	S	S	S ....
T	T	T	T ....
U	U	U	U ....
V	V	V	V ....
W	W	W	W ....
X	X	X	X ....
Y	Y	Y	Y ....
Z	Z	Z	Z ....

This list was compiled by ....

This list was compiled by ....

This list was compiled by ....

This list was compiled by ....

Characters in Chapter B[1]

Select from the choices the best description for the designated character. Be ready to explain your choice.

F	fun	fearful	fussy
E	edgy	eager	excited
R	rich	rude	respectful
N	normal	nice	nervous

E	energetic	excited	eager
L	likeable	lots of laughs	lovely
S	short	self-serving	sweet
A	ambitious	arrogant	angry

G	gift-giving	giant-like	gangly
O	opinionated	open	odd
L	likeable	lots of laughs	listener
I	intelligent	individual	irksome
A	angry	athletic	able
T	thoughtful	tense	tongue-tied
H	hasty	horrible	huge

M	magnificent	monstrous	middle-of-the-road
I	industrious	insistent	ineffectual
Z	zingy	zippy	zero
A	average	angry	agitated
S	soothing	sweet	soft
H	harsh	happy	hopeful
E	enthusiastic	earnest	effective

WonderWord 3

Chapter B[1] ~ Level: *super easy*

Directions for words are ➡ ⬅ ⬆ ⬇ ↗ ↘ ↗ ↖

H	E	H	S	A	Y	F
T	J	L	I	N	E	S
A	M	O	S	R	D	P
I	O	B	N	A	C	O
L	R	A	C	E	M	R
O	E	U	L	A	S	T
G	I	A	N	T	S	S

Find the following words:

- Ashe
- Elsa
- Fern
- Goliath
- Jones
- McDey

- sports
- last
- giants
- more
- run

There is one left-over letter. What is it? ....

Vocabulary in Chapter B[1]

1. **accusation** — a charge of wrongdoing
2. **compliant** — willing to be obedient
3. **etching** — a design on metal or glass
4. **ineffectual** — powerless
5. **innate** — existing in a person from birth
6. **spiteful** — full of a desire to injure another person
7. **suppress** — hold back or down; do away with
8. **tarnished** — a dull coating on metal
9. **thistledown** — the silky fluff of a thistle; like a dandelion

Identify the character on the left:

(1) Elsa
(2) Goliath Jones
(3) Mrs Ashe
(4) Freutim
(5) Uller

Explain your choice:
_____
_____
_____

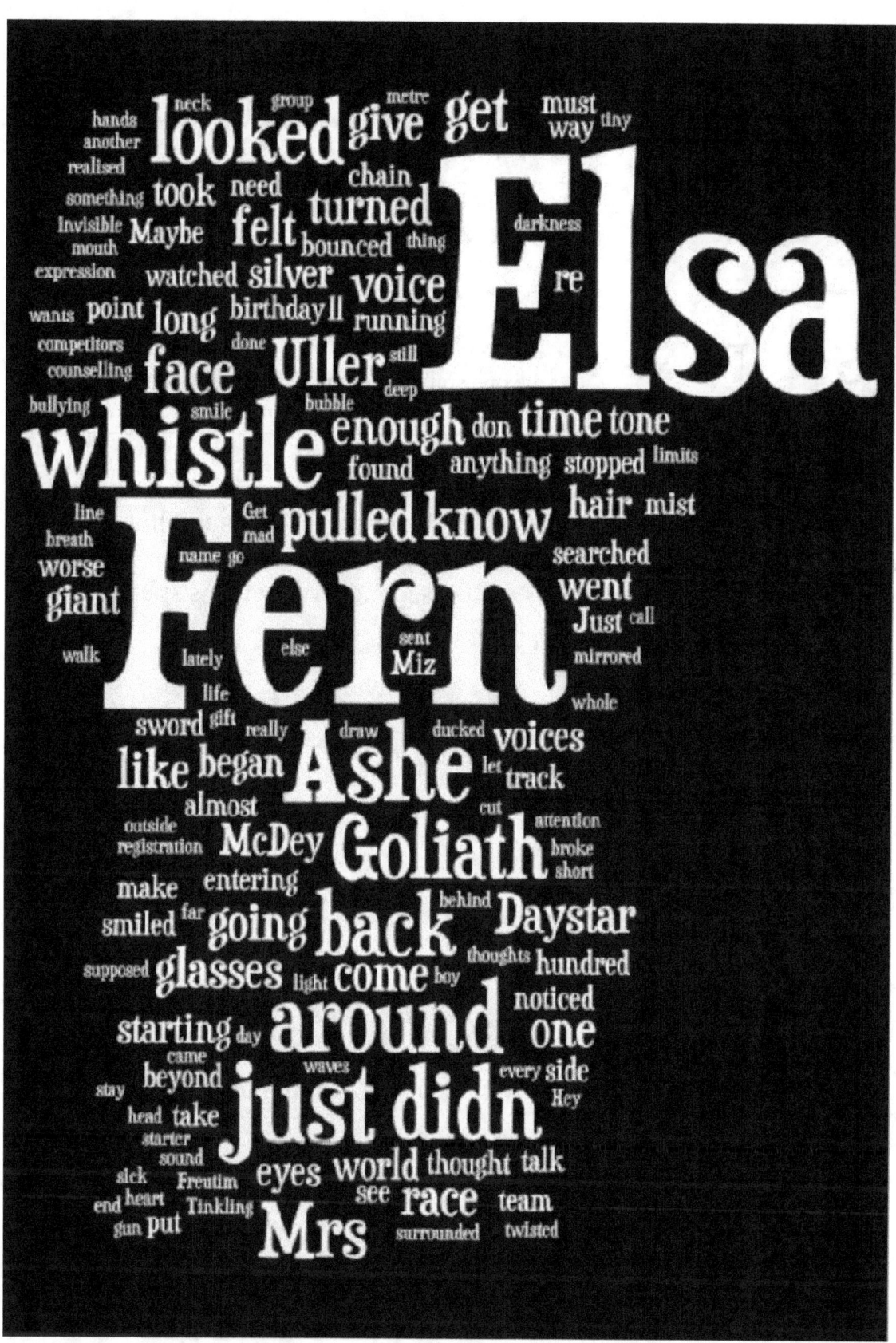

This is a wordcloud for Chapter B[1]. Write a description of yourself and make a wordcloud from it at a website like *Wordle*. Be sure to use your own name instead of 'I' so your name will appear as the most prominent element.

Teachers please note: Javascript plugin is needed to access the Wordle site. If this is disabled, students may not be able to complete this exercise. Please note the FAQs at Wordle regarding displays of inappropriate wordclouds on the site.

Speed Racers

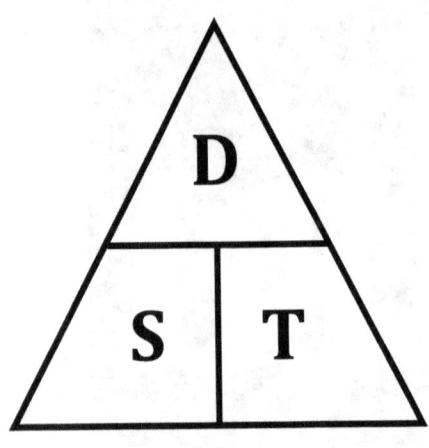

Use the diagram on the left to find any of speed (s), distance (d) or time (t)

If the one you want to know is on the top, you multiply by the two on the same level. D = S × T

If the one you want to know is on the bottom, you divide the others. S = D ÷ T or T = D ÷ S

Example 1: Usain Bolt can run the 100 metre sprint in 9.58 seconds. What is his speed?

Answer:

S = D ÷ T

   = 100 ÷ 9.58

   = 10.44 m/s

Example 2: Michael Johnson can run a 400 metre race in 43.18 seconds. What is his speed?

Answer:

S = D ÷ T

   = 400 ÷ 43.18

   = 9.26 m/s

Questions:

1. Elsa can run 100 metres in 11.5 seconds. What is her speed? How does it compare with Usain Bolt and Michael Johnson?

2. Goliath Jones can run 500 metres in 50.1 seconds. What is his speed? Who is fastest of Usain Bolt, Michael Johnson and Goliath?

3. If Goliath could keep up this speed for 1500 metres, how long would it take him to run that distance?

4. Fern can run 400 metres in 59.9 seconds. What is her speed? How does it compare with Elsa and Goliath?

5. If Usain Bolt could keep up a consistent speed for 1 minute, how far would he go?

6. If Usain Bolt could keep up a consistent speed for 1 hour, how far would he go?

7. If Goliath Jones maintained the same speed, how long would it take him to run 100 metres? Would this be a record?

ORDER THE EVENTS 1

Order the events which occur on sportsday at Fern's school

1	Fern jogs off the running track and leaves the school.
2	Snowflakes argue over copyright.
3	Fern realises the gift Elsa gave her came from Goliath.
4	Fern sees a giant with thistledown hair.
5	Elsa sends a text to Fern.
6	Fern is bullied by Elsa into entering a race for the Green Team.
7	A snow–white bubble captures Fern.
8	Mrs Ashe asks to see Elsa in her counselling room about bullying.
9	Prefects are sent to find Fern.
10	Fern enters the 1500 m race.

True or false?

Statement	True	False
Three prefects are sent to find Fern when she leaves the running track.		
Fern enters the 100 metre sprint for the Blue Team.		
Goliath Jones is the fastest runner in the school.		
Elsa is short, dark-haired and wears glasses with thick lenses.		
Mrs Ashe invites Fern and Elsa to discuss their differences.		
Fern hears two giants talking about the King Who Guards the Gate.		
Fern sends Elsa a text message to ask about sports day.		
Goliath is a midget, also known as 'Mouse' and 'Hobbit'.		

CLOZE ~ 2

It is sports _____ at Fern's school.

Fern is tricked into running a _____ which is _____ metres long, so that the _____ team can gain _____ for her entry. She realises her step-sister _____ has given her a silver _____ as a gift for her _____. However, Elsa was just giving it away in order to insult _____ Jones.

When Fern puts it in her mouth and _____ on it, she sees two _____. One is called Freutim and the other is called _____. They are talking about their search for the King _____.
Fern thinks she is hallucinating.

The school chaplain, Mrs _____, tells _____ she wants to see her about bullying. During the race, Fern decides to _____.

Characters in Chapter C¹

Select from the choices the best description for the designated character. Be ready to explain your choice.

A	angry	affectionate	abrasive
N	nasty	normal	nervous
S	sick	slippery	serving
E	escaping	Excited	exhausted
Y	young	Yellow	yielding

G	generous	greasy	good
R	rude	respectful	rickety
A	amiable	argumentative	aggressive
T	thoughtful	tearful	teasing
I	independent	iron-willed	impish
A	angry	affectionate	abrasive
N	nasty	normal	nervous

M	merry	mild	moody
A	angry	affectionate	abrasive
U	understanding	unhappy	urgent
R	royal	regular	rebellious
T	thoughtful	tearful	testy
Z	zany	zesty	zippy

B	beautiful	bossy	bright
A	angry	affectionate	abrasive
R	rude	respectful	rickety
B	boring	buck-teethed	bad-tempered
I	independent	iron-willed	impish
Z	zany	zingy	zippy
C	careful	considerate	cutting
A	amiable	argumentative	aggressive

Colour in Ansey below. Add a background. Choose from:
- the mountains where he first spotted the King's Shield
- the Mistmurk swamp where he was caught
- the throneroom in Auberon

Choosing **Names** 2: *Star-names*

The horses in Chapter A[1] and C[1] of *Daystar* are named after stars in the constellation of Orion the hunter. Rigel is a dazzling blue–white star and Mintaka is a star in Orion's Belt.

Research time:

1. Explain what a constellation is: ....
2. Find the common names of three other stars in Orion (http://en.wikipedia.org/wiki/List_of_stars_in_Orion):
    (i)   ....
    (ii)   ....
    (iii)   ....
3. Write down the proper scientific names of the three you have chosen:
    (i)   ....
    (ii)   ....
    (iii)   ....
4. Find a picture of the Horsehead Nebula and explain what a nebula is:

   ....

5. Find (or draw) a picture of the constellation Orion and mark the following on it: Rigel, Mintaka, Horsehead Nebula, Great Orion Nebula, Orion's Belt, Orion's Sword.

6. The story of Orion comes from Greek mythology. Summarise it in a few sentences.
   (http://www.rmg.co.uk/stories-of-the-skies/orion)

   ....
   ....
   ....
   ....
   ....
   ....

7. Make up a story of your own about animals that come from the stars. It could be an alien cat or an inter-galactic dog or a trans-dimensional bat. Or any other animal you choose. If you find difficulty choosing a name for your star-traveller, take seven scrabble tiles and re-arrange them to make up a name.

WonderWord 4

_ _ _ _ _ _ _ _ _ d

Chapter C^1 ~ Level: *medium*

Directions for words could be any of ⇒ ⇐ ⇑ ⇓ ↗ ↘ ↗ ↖

M	B	A	R	B	I	Z	C	A	C
A	G	K	Q	D	S	N	S	U	H
U	N	I	U	L	E	E	E	B	A
R	I	S	E	O	H	L	R	E	M
T	K	B	E	B	C	T	V	R	B
Z	H	I	N	Y	N	S	A	O	E
V	G	R	A	T	I	A	N	N	R
O	G	D	O	H	F	C	T	I	L
W	L	E	E	N	K	R	S	A	A
P	R	I	N	C	E	Y	T	P	I
H	O	O	C	A	P	T	A	I	N

Find the following words:

- Maurtz
- Ansey
- Tybold
- Barbizca
- Gratian
- King
- Queen
- Chamberlain
- Servants
- Bird
- Finches
- Auberon
- Castle
- Throne
- Prince
- Captain
- Pain
- Kneel
- Vow
- Cry

The leftover letters complete the title & spell out Ansey's hope for the future.

Vocabulary in Chapter C[1]

1. **aftershock** — a small earthquake or tremor that follows a major one
2. **battlements** — defensive wall or elevation on a castle
3. **black ice** — thin, often invisible, sheet of ice formed by freezing mist
4. **collective** — combined together; forming a whole
5. **conspiracy** — unlawful or secret plan devised by two or more plotters
6. **contradiction** — denial; statement of the opposite
7. **deceive** — mislead by a false statement
8. **forswear** — reject under oath
9. **gullible** — easily cheated
10. **inauguration** — ceremony to begin something
11. **notorious** — widely and unfavorably known
12. **manipulate** — to influence skilfully, often in an unfair way
13. **portcullis** — a strong grating made to block passage through a gateway
14. **precarious** — uncertain, unstable or insecure
15. **precipice** — a cliff with a very steep overhanging face
16. **predatory** — operating with selfish motives
17. **scree** — steep mass of stones on the side of a mountain
18. **sequester** — remove into a solitary place
19. **switchbacks** — hairpin curves on a road
20. **tattooing** — drumming

21. **taunt** — mock or insult

22. **treasonable** — involved in trying to overthrow the government

23. **tyranny** — unjustly severe government or ruler

24. **unwarranted** — not authorised

25. **usurp** — seize or hold without legal right

26. **venom** — poison

27. **vigilant** — keenly watchful, alert for danger

28. **viperous** — like a poisonous snake

29. **whelp** — the young of a dog, wolf, lion, bear; or an impudent boy

Identify the character on the right:

(1) Ansey

(2) Gratian

(3) Barbizca

(4) Maurtz

(5) Chamberlain

Explain your choice:

_____

_____

_____

From the description of Castle Auberon in Chapter C[1], draw in the outer courtyard and surrounds. Include finches, swans, peacocks and geese in your drawing. Add an extension to the castle of your own design.

Vocabulary in Chapter D[1]

1.	**ambience**	mood, tone or atmosphere
2.	**anomalous**	not fitting anything familiar
3.	**atrocious**	extremely wicked, cruel or brutal
4.	**belligerent**	war–like
5.	**brusque**	abrupt in manner
6.	**defect**	fault or imperfection
7.	**duality**	double state
8.	**multi-dimensional**	more than one dimension
9.	**precipitate**	hasten the appearance of
10.	**resplendence**	splendour
11.	**rite–of–passage**	ceremony to pass from childhood to adulthood
12.	**scrutinise**	examine with careful attention
13.	**self-deprecating**	undervaluing yourself
14.	**silhouette**	outline or dark image of an object
15.	**simultaneous**	two (or more) events occurring at the same time
16.	**theoretical**	existing only in theory, not in practice
17.	**unabashed**	not ashamed or apologetic
18.	**willy-nilly**	in a disorganised or unplanned manner

Which of the pictures above is a silhouette?

POINT OF VIEW

When Fern meets the 'White Three of the White Tree', the story is told through her eyes. How would it change if you saw it from the point of view of one of the other characters in the scene?

Choose one of them—

- the owl Boody (Boudicca's Chariot)
- the fox Hector
- the fawn Ginevra (Ginevra–'ayelet–hashachar)

and tell the story of their meeting Fern from that perspective.

_____

_____

_____

_____

_____

_____

_____

C*L*O*Z*E* ~ 3

The white _____ which surrounded Fern has taken her to another dimension.

Under the White _____, she meets the White Three: Boody, a tiny white _____; _____, a small white fox and _____ –'ayelet–hashachar, a white _____.

The white fox is waiting for a _____ to come by, and expects he will ask him to help save the _____. So he wants Fern to go in case she's spoiling his chance to fulfil his _____. When the fox realises that there are strange little plates over Fern's _____, all the animals come to the conclusion that she comes from another _____. They realise their world is threatened with destruction and Fern has been brought through because she is the 'Perfect _____.'

Boody falls in love with the idea of _____.

Vocabulary in Chapter E[1]

1. **apportion** — to distribute
2. **armoire** — a large wardrobe or moveable cupboard with doors and shelves
3. **baleful** — full of menace
4. **balmy** — mild and refreshing
5. **careening** — swaying or tipping while in motion
6. **caterwaul** — utter long wailing cry (like a cat)
7. **dejected** — depressed or disheartened
8. **enlistment** — time for military service
9. **harrumph** — cough deliberately
10. **hoarse** — husky or harsh sound from throat
11. **integrity** — honesty or wholeness
12. **malice** — desire to injure or harm
13. **manticore** — a legendary monster with a man's head, horns, a lion's body and the tail of a dragon or, sometimes, a scorpion
14. **minstrel** — a musician, singer or poet
15. **oriel window** — a bay window projecting from a wall
16. **peeved** — annoyed
17. **pensive** — thoughtful
18. **phosphorescent** — emitting light at low temperatures
19. **prominent** — standing out to be seen easily

20.	**recruitment**	the act of enlisting a person
21.	**squire**	a young person of noble birth who served a knight
22.	**strafe**	to attack from the air with repetitive fire
23.	**thwart**	to oppose successfully
24.	**tippets**	long narrow parts of sleeves or hoods
25.	**tournament**	a trial of skill
26.	**venison**	the meat of a deer
27.	**virtuoso**	person with special knowledge or skill

Assonance: *words that sound alike*

The words *horse, hoarse, oars, haws* and *awes* are assonances because their vowel sounds are alike. They don't rhyme but they have a similar sound. Match up each correctly to its meaning and in the first column, write a rhyming word.

	horse	paddles using in the rowing of a boat
	hoarse	causes wonder and amazement
	oars	a four-legged animal used for riding
	hawse	harsh or husky sound in the throat
	awes	part of a ship's bow with openings for cables

WINDOWS

(1) In the pictures below, identify the **oriel** window.

(2) Which character in the story has an oriel window in his or her bedroom?

(3) Research the following kinds of windows and sketch them on the back of this sheet: Gothic, Rose, Romanesque, Transom, Hopper, Jalousie, Casement.

(A)

(B)

(C)

(D)

WINDOW WONDERLAND

Choose a particular window shape and create a fantasy window. Make sure the window is open, so you can see outside. Decorate the window with coloured sequins or glitter and draw your own fantasy landscape beyond. What would you see? Describe it in a paragraph.

_____

_____

_____

WonderWord 5

A Tale of Two _ _ _ _ _ _ _ _

Chapter E[1] ~ Level: *medium*

Directions for words could be any of ⇒ ⇐ ⇑ ⇓ ⇗ ⇘ ⇗ ⇖

B	H	A	W	F	E	L	L	P	V	R
W	U	M	U	C	H	E	D	E	I	I
O	S	T	O	A	D	L	R	L	R	R
D	W	T	T	L	N	D	A	B	C	E
N	O	H	O	E	W	N	Y	M	O	V
I	R	G	P	A	R	A	T	A	N	I
W	D	I	R	T	M	C	R	R	T	R
L	M	F	A	N	C	E	U	B	I	D
E	A	F	C	U	N	R	O	P	U	N
I	S	I	T	A	O	E	C	P	M	O
R	T	L	I	T	Y	B	O	L	D	M
O	E	C	C	A	R	R	I	A	G	E
S	R	A	E	S	A	I	B	O	T	D

Find the following words:

- Buttercup
- Candle
- Courtyard
- Oriel window
- Dwarf
- Fight
- Swordmaster
- Practice
- Vircontium
- Tybold
- Taunt
- Carriage
- Demon
- Driver
- Cliff
- Bramble
- Arena
- Hawfell
- Much
- Tobias
- Poem
- Toad
- Gold
- Actor

The leftover letters complete the title.

Alluring **Alliteration** Always Appeals

According to Candle, one of the great dwarf poets said: **Bitter bulbs breed baleful blossoms**. But he didn't say it quickly.

Try to say it quickly. Time yourself and see how long it takes you to say it properly without stumbling over the words.

Other examples of alliteration are:

- Peter Piper picked a peck of pickled pepper.
- She sells sea shells by the sea shore.

Try to say these quickly. Time yourself and see how long it takes you to say it properly without stumbling over the words.

1. What is alliteration? ....

2. Write down your name or nickname: ....

3. Using this as your base, create an alliterative sentence to describe yourself.

   ....

   ....

4. How fast can you say this sentence? ....

5. Choose one of the characters from *Daystar*: ....

6. Write down an alliterative sentence to describe that character.

   ....

   ....

7. How fast can you say this sentence? ....

ORDER THE EVENTS 2

Order the events which occur in Candle's story of the demon driver

1	The coach reached the Fyrzentsou border
2	The driver tried a cloud-shadow deception to throw off the pursuit
3	The tutors were told they had to flee for their lives
4	The back wheels of the coach fell off
5	The driver took the coach down the Face of Harrowfell
6	Old Greywhiskers found a bee-keeping outfit
7	Much was banged on the head by Greywhiskers for saying, 'Shh!'
8	Old Greywhiskers thought a new bee species had been discovered
9	Harper smacked a guard's head with the butterfly net
10	Old Greywhiskers sang a bee-keeping song

True or false?

Statement	True	False
Ansey has always wanted to be a knight		
The queen rewarded Ansey's tutors with gold		
Candle likes eating toffee-covered grapes		
Gratian knows the secret of wolf's-tail clouds		
The king agreed to allow Ansey to be a squire		
Gratian is one of Ansey's tutors		
Tybold is a dwarf and is Candle's son		
Ansey is happy that all his tutors have gone		
The demon driver was Captain Gratian		

Vocabulary in Chapter F[1]

1.	**balm**	fragrant ointment
2.	**bedraggled**	limp and dirty
3.	**chapbook**	small book
4.	**conspicuous**	easily seen
5.	**consternation**	sudden dismay
6.	**deft**	skilful or clever
7.	**diligent**	constant in effort
8.	**discreet**	careful in behaviour or words
9.	**dispel**	drive off
10.	**elicit**	draw out
11.	**gawp**	stare with the mouth open
12.	**gilded**	covered in gold
13.	**indignant**	feeling upset at something unjust or insulting
14.	**inordinately**	uncontrolled
15.	**jerkin**	close-fitting short coat
16.	**lax**	careless
17.	**lotion**	soothing liquid
18.	**parquetry**	interlocking design of wooden floorwork
19.	**pavilion**	decorated tent
20.	**pennant**	long tapering flag
21.	**pennon**	tapering, triangular or swallow-tailed flag

22.	**pirouette**	whirling on toes
23.	**potion**	a drink with medical properties
24.	**poultice**	a soft, moist mass of cloth, bread and herbs used medically
25.	**preoccupied**	engrossed in thought
26.	**reparation**	making amends for a wrong
27.	**ruddy**	reddish
28.	**subtle**	requiring discernment
29.	**troubadour**	a wandering singer

In the picture below, draw in the following:

(1) a pavilion with a pennon flying from it
(2) a thin pennant trailing from a knight's helm

WonderWord 6

Chapter E[1] ~ Level: *medium*

Directions for words could be any of ⇒ ⇐ ⇑ ⇓ ↗ ↘ ↗ ↘

K	N	I	G	H	T	S	O	F	R	E	N	O	W	N
Q	U	Y	S	T	E	I	N	J	A	N	P	R	S	I
A	D	S	H	I	E	L	D	O	R	L	R	E	Q	N
T	N	G	O	S	E	V	S	U	M	I	O	C	U	T
T	E	A	N	W	C	E	P	S	O	S	P	R	A	E
A	F	R	O	O	N	R	E	T	U	T	H	U	D	G
C	E	G	U	R	A	K	A	O	R	M	E	I	R	R
K	D	E	R	D	L	A	R	M	S	E	C	T	O	I
T	O	U	R	N	A	M	E	N	T	N	Y	S	N	T
E	N	E	M	I	E	S	R	J	O	T	U	N	S	Y

Find the following words:

- Knights of Renown
- Enlistment
- Squadron
- Quystein
- Ysgarde
- Tournament
- Silver
- Shield
- Honour
- Prophecy
- Attack

- Defend
- Sword
- Lance
- Spear
- Joust
- Armour
- Arms
- Enemies
- Jotuns
- Recruits
- Integrity

How many leftover letters are there?
What are the leftover letters the initials of?

Choosing Names 3: Dwarf Names

Here are the names of the dwarves mentioned in *Daystar*:
Bramble, Candle, Humble, Kindle, Nobble, Puddle, Rubble, Toddle and Wobble.

Look carefully at the names to find the pattern and common element, then divide this mixed group of dwarves and giants into the right categories:

Bubble, Bokran, Bumble, Crumble, Dynn, Etin, Fumble, Jumble, Mangle, Mingle, Mobylt, Mumble, Nemora, Scoby, Stubble, Thuz, Titan, Tumble, Yulye.

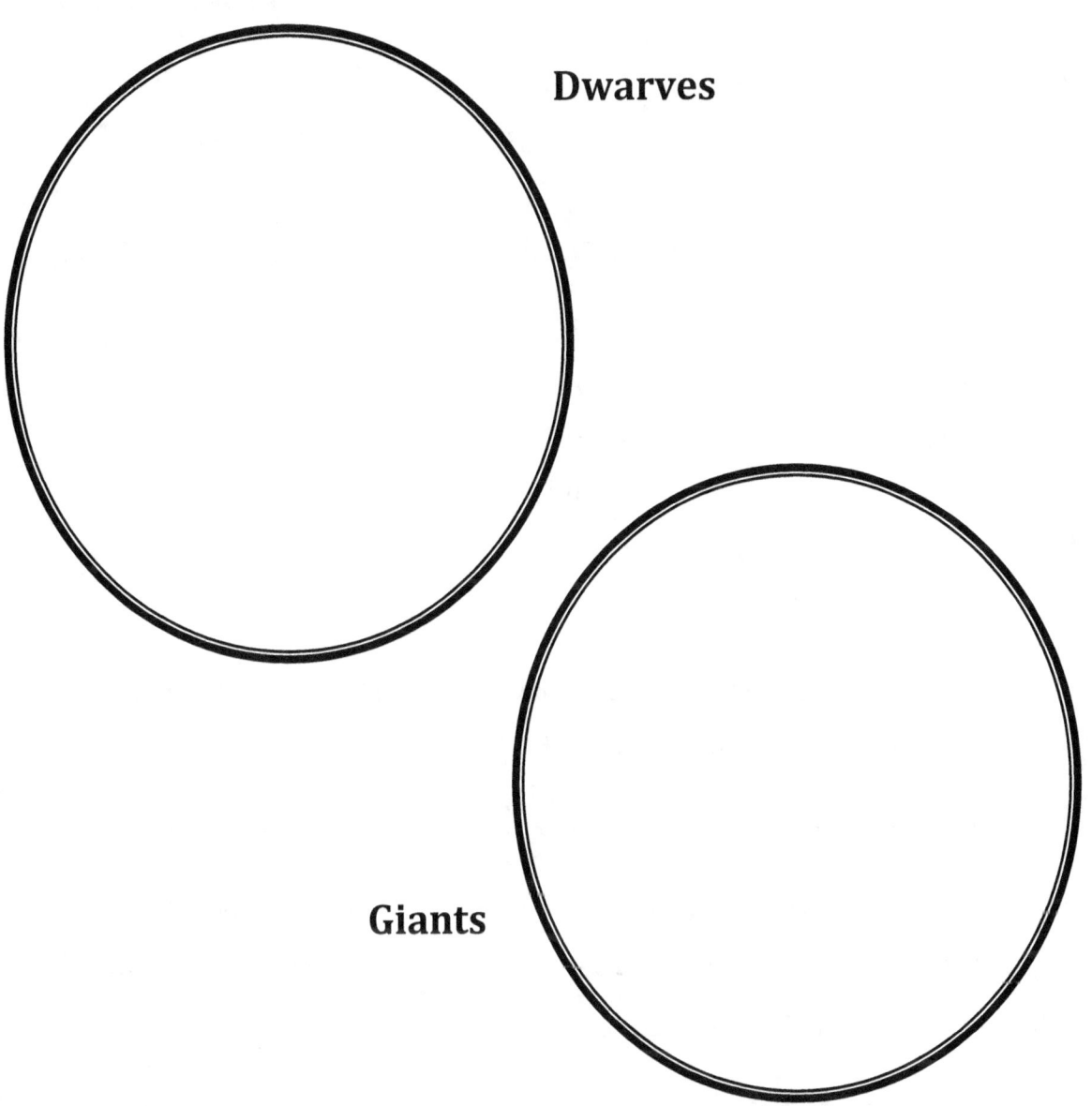

Make up names for seven more dwarves, using the pattern and common element:

....

ENDORSEMENTS

Here's what three dwarves said about *Daystar*:

'Adorable, agreeable, commendable, delectable, unforgettable!'

*****Nobble**, dwarf escort*

'Impeccable, invincible, incomparable, irresistible!'

*****Wobble**, dwarf escort*

'Noble!'

*****Stubble**, Commander of the Fifth Dwarf Legion*

1. Circle the words their dwarf friends would have used to keep to the same pattern:

Capable	Mysterious	Suitable
Curious	Monumental	Terrible
Magnificent	Notable	Terrific
Marvellous	Sensible	Unusual

2. Find another word of your own that keeps to the pattern. _____

3. Make up a new pattern of names that end with "*–ful*". Find a race of mythical creatures to give this set of names.

   _____   _____   _____

4. Choose a suffix (word ending) of your own. Perhaps it could be "*–ment*" or "*–less*". What does your suffix mean? _____ What are three words with your suffix in it? _____ _____ _____

5. Choose a prefix (word start) of your own. Perhaps it could be "*pre–*" or "*un–*". What does your prefix mean? _____ What are three words with your prefix in it? _____ _____ ____

Vocabulary in Chapter G[1]

1. **agenda** — a list of things to be done
2. **bamboozle** — get the better of someone by trickery
3. **deign** — behave in a superior way
4. **genocidal** — deliberate killing of an entire national, political or ethnic group
5. **incite** — to stir or urge
6. **induce** — to produce or cause
7. **interdiction** — a law forbidding a certain action
8. **intermittent** — alternatively stopping and starting again
9. **jackboots** — a person who is a bully
10. **lanky** — ungracefully thin
11. **mesmerise** — fascinate or hypnotise
12. **patronising** — behaving in an offensive, superior manner
13. **rearguard** — a detachment of soldiers sent to the rear
14. **sentient** — conscious
15. **sneer** — smile in a way that shows scorn
16. **spontaneous** — resulting from a sudden impulse
17. **surcoat** — an outer garment worn over armour, often with heraldic arms on it
18. **talons** — claws

19.	**tier**	a set of rows rising behind each other
20.	**ulterior**	intentionally hidden
21.	**unadorned**	without any decoration
22.	**unblemished**	without any faults or blemishes
23.	**unkempt**	untidy
24.	**unsheathed**	without a cover or sheath
25.	**ventriloquist**	a person who is able to produce sounds that seem to come from another source
26.	**vicious**	spiteful

Visual Comprehension

Is the sword held by the knight in the picture at the right *sheathed* or *unsheathed*?

Is the *surcoat* worn by the knight *adorned* or *unadorned*?

Is the knight *unkempt*?

Is the knight's helmet *blemished* or *unblemished*?

Choosing **Names** 4

Chapters A¹—G¹~ Level: *difficult*

Write an acrostic poem to describe these characters:

A _____	B _____	D _____
N _____	O _____	A _____
S _____	O _____	L _____
E _____	D _____	L _____
Y _____	Y _____	A _____
		N _____

F _____	H _____	G _____
E _____	E _____	I _____
R _____	C _____	N _____
N _____	T _____	E _____
	O _____	V _____
	R _____	R _____
		A _____

ACROSTIC Challenges:

B _____	A _____	G _____
O _____	N _____	I _____
U _____	C _____	N _____
D _____	E _____	E _____
I _____	L _____	V _____
C _____	I _____	R _____
C _____	N _____	A _____
A' _____		
S _____	B _____	'A _____
	E _____	Y _____
C _____	D _____	E _____
H _____	W _____	L _____
A _____	Y _____	E _____
R _____	R _____	T _____
I _____		
O _____	C _____	H _____
T _____	A _____	A _____
	I _____	S _____
		H _____
		A _____
		C _____
		H _____
		A _____
		R _____

Super ACROSTIC Challenge: *your own name*

WonderWord 7

Chapter G[1] ~ Level: *easy*

Directions for words could be any of ⇒ ⇐ ⇑ ⇓ ↘ ↘ ↗ ↙

M	A	D	M	E	R	R	Y
G	R	A	N	S	E	Y	D
I	O	L	F	E	R	N	O
N	T	L	T	E	N	T	O
E	C	A	S	O	U	L	B
V	E	N	T	R	A	E	H
R	H	C	A	N	D	L	E
A	G	N	I	L	A	E	H

Find the following words:

- Ansey
- Boody
- Candle
- Dallan
- Fern
- Ginevra
- Hector
- Madmerry
- tent
- soul
- heart
- healing

How many leftover letters are there? ....

ORDER THE EVENTS 3

Order the events which occur in Uller's abduction of Ansey

1	A bellow is heard from the Tourney Ground
2	Uller reveals he has a contract to kill two princes
3	Candle tells Ansey to run
4	Uller introduces his messengers, the two ravens
5	Tybold identifies Ansey and suggests he'd make a better hostage
6	Uller gives Ansey a collar of fine silver-grey chainmail
7	Ansey starts to shiver with cold
8	Tybold is seen struggling in the giant's left hand
9	Ansey wakes up and discovers he is in a swamp
10	Ansey is scooped up by the frost giant
11	The Knights of Renown surround the frost giant
12	Uller tries to pump Ansey for information about Prince Emyr
13	Ansey spots the finches making a trail across the sky
14	Uller promises to kill Ansey if ever he sees him again
15	Uller forgets his sword

(1) Name the swamp pictured on the left.

_____

(2) Name the type of bird in the picture.

_____

(3) What are the names of the two birds?

_____

Page | 58

Vocabulary in Chapter A²

1.	**abduct**	carry away by force
2.	**assassin**	a paid murderer
3.	**buckler**	a shield or other form of protection
4.	**civil**	respectful
5.	**cosseted**	treated as a pet
6.	**flinch**	draw back or shrink
7.	**gnarled**	bent or twisted
8.	**petrified**	paralysed by fear
9.	**sanctuary**	a sacred or holy place
10.	**speculative**	based on guesswork
11.	**surfeit**	excess, too much
12.	**molested**	bothered or ill-treated
13.	**vegetarian**	a person who does not eat meat

In this picture, draw in the method the finches use to point out the direction the frost giant headed when he abducted Ansey.

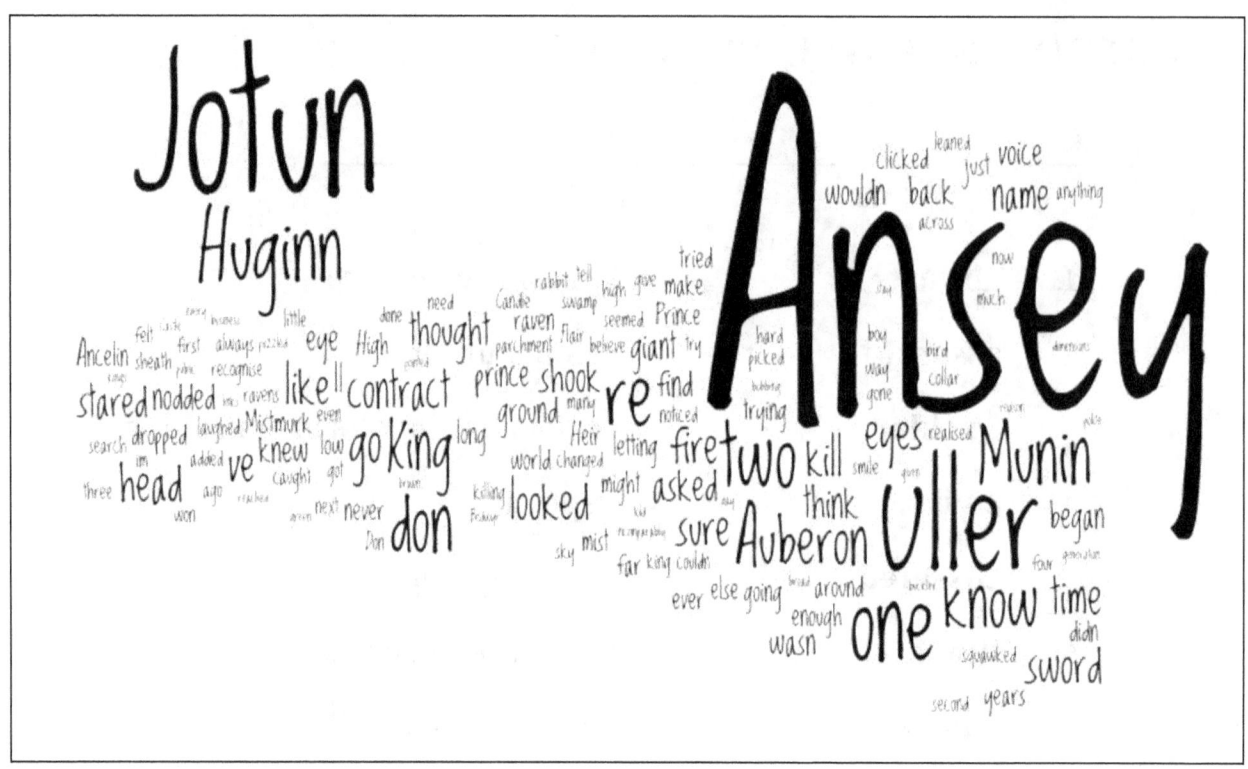

Wordcloud 2

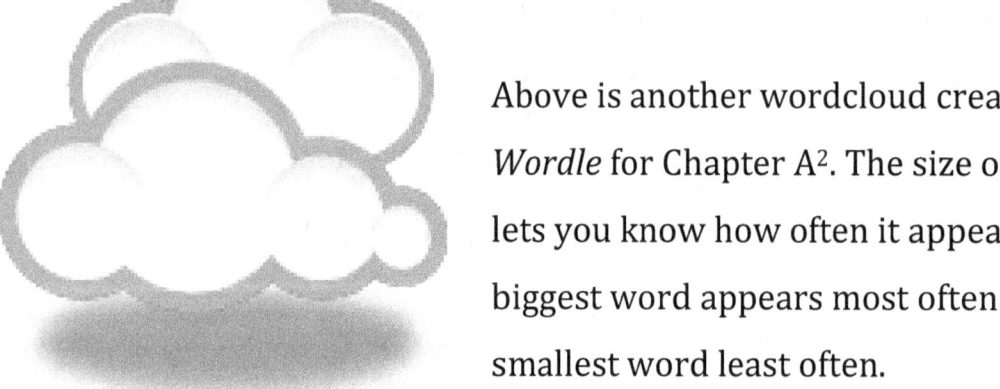

Above is another wordcloud created at *Wordle* for Chapter A². The size of the words lets you know how often it appears. The biggest word appears most often and the smallest word least often.

Create your own wordcloud for the story you wrote about the animals that come from the stars. (Chapter C¹ on page 27)

Cut and paste your words into the text box *Wordle* and then randomise the picture until it's one you like. Print it out.

WonderWord 8

FEATURE

Chapters A² and B² ~ Level: *easy* → *medium*

Directions for words could be any of ⇒ ⇐ ⇑ ⇓ ↗ ↘ ↗ ↘

M	G	M	L	E	G	I	R	B	B
F	I	U	F	A	W	N	R	O	R
I	N	N	I	G	U	H	O	U	A
N	E	I	T	C	R	D	T	D	H
C	V	N	Y	A	Y	R	C	I	C
H	R	E	V	N	K	A	E	C	A
E	A	E	L	W	O	A	H	C	H
S	N	D	R	I	B	P	T	A	S
F	C	H	A	R	I	O	T	'	A
O	'	A	Y	E	L	E	T	S	H
X	S	E	S	R	O	H	U	R	E

The leftover letters form the missing part of the title.

- Ginevra
- 'Ayelet
- Hector
- Rigel
- Mintaka
- Munin
- Huginn
- Hashachar
- Boudicca's
- Bird
- Finches
- Horses
- Raven
- Pony
- Chariot
- Boody
- Fox
- Fawn
- Owl

WonderWord 9

Chapters A² and B² ~ Level: *easy* → *medium*

Directions for words could be any of ⇒ ⇐ ⇑ ⇓ ↗ ↘ ↗ ↖

P	R	I	N	C	E	K	I	L	L	E	R
A	P	F	H	F	I	R	E	D	R	I	B
N	E	P	R	O	A	U	L	L	E	R	E
C	E	R	H	V	S	M	U	N	I	N	D
E	L	I	E	U	C	T	S	A	O	R	W
L	S	N	E	A	G	S	A	W	I	C	Y
I	S	C	I	M	U	I	S	G	O	O	R
N	S	E	T	G	Y	M	N	S	E	R	I
A	N	S	T	C	A	R	T	N	O	C	D
F	Y	R	Z	E	N	T	S	O	U	M	T

The leftover letters spell out something about Uller.

- Uller
- Princekiller
- Mistmurk
- Fire
- Ancelin
- Bedwyr
- Cai
- Emyr
- Moss
- Ravens
- Hostage
- Munin
- Huginn
- Contract
- Roast
- Sleep
- Sword
- Icy
- Bird
- Guy
- Fyrzentsou
- Princes

Teacher's Notes 2 from the Author:

On Naming

You may wish to refer to other children's books where naming plays a significant role:

- In Glenda Millard's *The Naming of Tishkin Silk*, the naming of the Silk children is deferred until they are one year old. In *The Tender Moments of Saffron Silk*, the special naming day book each of the children is given is highlighted.

- In Andrew Lansdown's *With My Knife*, Colyn dreams that the dragon chases him to his special place by the river where it learned his name from his carving in the tree. In the sequel *Dragonfox*, Yasni uses the true names given to creatures at the dawn of time to call them to attack the dragon.

- In Rebecca Anderson's *Rebel*, the dark queen Jasmine holds power over her subjects through her knowledge of their true names. The white stone held by the Children of Rhys has the ability to impart a new name to anyone who holds it.

- In Madeleine L'Engle's *A Wind in the Door*, Meg discovers that naming casts out fear when she is confronted by the life-annihilating Un-namers, the Echthroi.

- In Ursula Le Guin's *A Wizard of Earthsea*, Ged has to find the name of the murderous phantom he has unleashed on his world before it can be overcome.

- In David Cornish's series *Monster Blood Tattoo*, Rossamünd's true nature is revealed by his name.

- In Julie Bertagna's *Exodus* and *Zenith*, the Treenesters who lived on the islands below the sky towers of New Mungo are named to commemorate suburbs in the drowned Scottish city of Glasgow.

- In Anne Hamilton's *Many-Coloured Realm*, escape from the goblin realm is only possible by telling the goblin king his true name—but not even he knows what it is. The elves in the story all hide their true names behind the words for rivers, regions and old towns.

MEANINGS FOR SELECTED NAMES

Ancelin:

Originally I chose this because I wanted a knightly name for the character. In my view nothing could be more evocative of a knight than the name Lancelot from the stories of king Arthur. However, I didn't want the name to be too obvious and I looked for ways to modify it. I discovered in The *Dictionary of First Names* that Ancel or Ancelin, meaning *servant*, is a variation of Lancelot. This was perfect for a boy who wanted to serve others through becoming a knight. His full name, Ancelin Bedwyr Cai, not only reflects the alphabetic theme hidden in the story but harks back to three of the most famous knights of the Round Table: Lancelot, Bedivere and Kay.

Ansey:

This nickname for Ancelin was a very fortunate choice. *The Great Australian and New Zealand Book of Baby Names* added the following information about Ancel and Ancelin: it could be from Latin and mean *servant*, but it could also be from German, *ansi*, and mean *a god*. Internet research on this enabled me to discover it was probably a variation of Acelin, meaning *noble, of high birth, a ruler*. I loved this because it gave the nickname two senses: a king and a servant. Just what I wanted.

Boody:

This nickname for the baby owl is an onomatopoeic name, reflecting the kind of hoot she makes. By happy chance, 'budi' is an Indonesian word meaning *wise one*. As owls are traditionally described as wise, this is a delightful but unplanned congruence.

Boudicca's Chariot:

This is Boody's full name. She is called after the war chariot with scything blades on its wheel used by the great British warrior queen of the first century, Boudicca (sometimes spelt Boadicea). She was supposed to grow up to be a warrior owl with lacerating talons just like those wicked scything blades.

In fact, nothing could be less appropriate when it comes to names than this. Boody doesn't run over anyone or cut anyone down. She is exceptionally gentle, except when protecting her friends. Or unless a matter of sunglasses is involved.

Cindurrah:

This is a personal invention. As far as I am aware, the name does not actually exist. (But I've been wrong before: see Uller below.) I based it on Ciddirah, mentioned in *Names from Here and Far: The New Holland Dictionary of Names*. The suggestion there, by no means certain, is that Ciddirah means *star-born*. I have assigned the meaning *star-shepherd* to Cindurrah.

Dallan:

An Irish name meaning *blind*. I chose it from *The Great Australian and New Zealand Book of Baby Names* for no other reason than the character in the story is visually impaired. Subsequently I discovered that the most famous bearer of the name was Dallan Forgaill, a blind Irish monk and chief of all the bards, who wrote the beautiful lorica ('breastplate song'), *Be Thou My Vision*. It is also, I have belatedly discovered, according to the book *Inishowen: Its History, Traditions & Antiquities Containing a Number of Original Documents with Numerous Notes from the Annals of the Four Masters and Other Sources* (isn't that a mouthful of a title?) a word signifying a *pillar* or a *standing stone*.

Emyr:

According to *The Great Australian and New Zealand Book of Baby Names*, this Welsh name means *honour*.

Fern:

On the surface, this simply means *fern, the green plant*. At first I thought this a tip of the hat to the girl in *Charlotte's Web*, but I eventually decided otherwise. I like *Charlotte's Web* but it certainly doesn't come even remotely close to being a favourite book of mine, so there had to be another reason hidden deep in my unconscious. I think that the name goes back to Welsh *vran* and that it is therefore meant to evoke a *wren* or a *robin*.

Ginevra-'ayelet-hashachar:

The name of the white baby fawn. According to *The Great Australian and New Zealand Book of Baby Names*, Ginevra is the Italian form of Jennifer or Guinevere, the name of King Arthur's queen in the stories of the knights of the Round Table. This is said to mean *white and fair* or *white wave*, although *Names from Here and Far: The New Holland Dictionary of Names* says it means *white and smooth*, and *Scottish Forenames* suggests *fair and yielding*. *Name Your Baby* says *white wave* or *white phantom*. Obviously there are many different opinions but the common elements are *white* and *fair*: two things that really describe Ginevra the fawn.

The last part of Ginevra's name is taken from the Hebrew phrase אַיֶּלֶת הַשַּׁחַר ('ayelet hashachar), meaning *gazelle of dawn*, a name of the morning star. Since she is a baby, she is rightly named by the others as the 'fawn of dawn'.

Hector:

I had real trouble naming the little white fox and my sister eventually chose this for me. There's a pun in his explanation of why he changed his name from Ector to Hector. He says he wanted something more aspirational. This has a double meaning. The term 'aspirant' refers to adding an 'h' at the front of a word. However, an aspirant is also someone who aspires or aims for something greater. Ector is a variant of Hector and is also a name from Arthurian legend: he is Kay's father and Arthur's foster-father. Hector is a Greek name meaning *hold fast*. He was a Trojan hero who was killed by the Greek warrior Achilles and dragged around the walls of Troy by his heels. Guess why Hector wears protective shoes?

Huginn and **Munin**:

These are names chosen from Norse mythology, as is Munin. These two ravens belong to Odin, the chief of the Norse gods, in the ancient legends of the North. Munin and Huginn are generally translated as *Thought* and *Memory*. However, the names have a much deeper and wider resonance than this restricted sense. They could also be translated as *Mind* and *Heart* or *Heart* and *Soul* or *Knowledge* and *Wisdom* or a combination.

Madmerry:

I thought I invented this name. So I was very disconcerted to find that Robert Graves suggests that Mad Merry is an alternative spelling for Maid Marian.

Uller:

I thought I'd invented this name too. I assigned it the meaning *winter*, since after all that fits a frost giant quite nicely. I was even more disconcerted than with Madmerry to discover it is a real name. And that it actually does mean *winter*! Its other meaning is *yew tree*. However the really disconcerting part was that I'd given Uller two ravens as spies and, on looking for names suitable for ravens, decided that the names of Odin's companions, Munin and Huginn, could hardly be bettered. That, as I turned out, was a classic understatement. What seemed random was far from it.

Uller is a name from Norse mythology and at once time he ruled in Odin's stead. Apparently Odin was once punished for practising black magic—the law applies even if you are king of the gods—and he was exiled from Asgard. While he was gone, Uller was given his throne. Nothing is mentioned about Uller having Odin's ravens. But it certainly isn't as random a choice as I thought. The legend of Uller is very fragmentary and although there is no mention of killing princes in it, I wouldn't be at all surprised if this was once part of it.

As Alan Garner wrote in his notes to *The Moon of Gomrath*: *The more I learn, the more I am convinced that there are no original stories. On several occasions I have 'invented' an incident, and then come across it in an obscure fragment of Hebridean lore, orally collected, and privately printed, a hundred years ago.*

As far as I am concerned, Garner is right. There are no original stories. There is nothing new under the sun. What I thought I had invented, I realised I had discovered. As far as I am concerned a writer is not so much a creator as an explorer blazing a trail across an as–yet undiscovered landscape.

Themes:

Peace
- not simply as an aftermath and goal of war, but more specifically as a virtue or an attitude which actively seeks to resolve conflict without violence

Hope
- that there is purpose in even the greatest disappointment and that all things work together for good to those called to achieve this purpose

Love
- beyond friendship and acceptance; a pledged relationship to always help and always protect each other; not a feeling but an action that expresses itself in courage, the sacrifice personal dreams and service to others

Grace
- the sudden appearance of unexpected gifts in the most unlikely way and the faith response which follows

Honour
- integrity of character; side-lining personal ambition to serve a greater good; keeping your word despite intense pressure to break it

Destiny
- a high calling on the life of an individual; not as an inexorable outworking of fate (as demonstrated by the fact one of the characters is a substitute) but as walking into the summoning of future

Seven
- Seven Days, Seven Children with names from Seven different Letters of the alphabet, Seven Powers, Seven Virtues, Seven Kingdoms, Seven Protectors of the Realm, Seven Cloaks, Seven Colours, Seven Musical Notes, Sevenfold Panoply: all of which are, in some sense, One. Not to mention 77777 words in the story itself. And 7 words in the title: *The Days are Numbered Book 1: Daystar*

Vocabulary in Chapter B²

1. **autistic** — abnormally self-absorbed
2. **a.s.a.p.** — abbreviation for *as soon as possible*
3. **belligerent** — war-like or aggressive
4. **canopy** — covering, usually of fabric; also the covering formed by the top leafy branches of a tree
5. **dejection** — depression or lowness of spirit
6. **effrontery** — shameless boldness
7. **flank** — side of an animal
8. **flippant** — disrespectful
9. **frazzled** — worn-out
10. **glacier** — an extended mass of ice formed by falling snow
11. **haunches** — part of the body around the hips
12. **heath** — wasteland overgrown with shrubs
13. **intentionally** — deliberately
14. **jeopardised** — put into danger
15. **leech-surgeons** — doctors who use blood-sucking leeches
16. **obstructive** — make difficult to pass
17. **pristine** — having its original perfection
18. **rendezvous** — meeting place
19. **self-imposed** — put upon yourself

20.	**snivelling**	cry with sniffling
21.	**spectre**	ghost
22.	**supernova**	brilliant exploding star
23.	**tremulous**	trembling from fear or nervousness
24.	**tumbrel**	a cart that can be tilted
25.	**vixen**	a female fox
26.	**vulpine**	fox-like

Vocabulary in Chapter C²

1.	**gloaming**	dusk or twilight
2.	**sedge**	rushes or grasses that grow in wet places

BIRDBRAINS

Match the bird to its correct name:

OWL	RAVEN	FINCH

Vocabulary in Chapter D²

1.	**arrogant**	insolently proud
2.	**beatific**	blissful
3.	**beetled**	moved quickly
4.	**citadel**	fortress that commands a city
5.	**englacial**	inside the ice of a glacier
6.	**devious**	shifty or crooked
7.	**futile**	unimportant
8.	**impertinent**	intrusive and rude
9.	**incensed**	made angry
10.	**mutinous**	rebellious
11.	**peter**	stop gradually
12.	**provocative**	incite or irritate
13.	**spasm**	spurt of energy, activity or muscle action
14.	**succumb**	give way to a greater force
15.	**tinderbox**	a box for holding fire-making equipment
16.	**vigilance**	state of being watchful
17.	**whisk**	move with rapid strokes

Choose from this vocabulary list a word to describe the fortified tower in the centre of this picture: ....

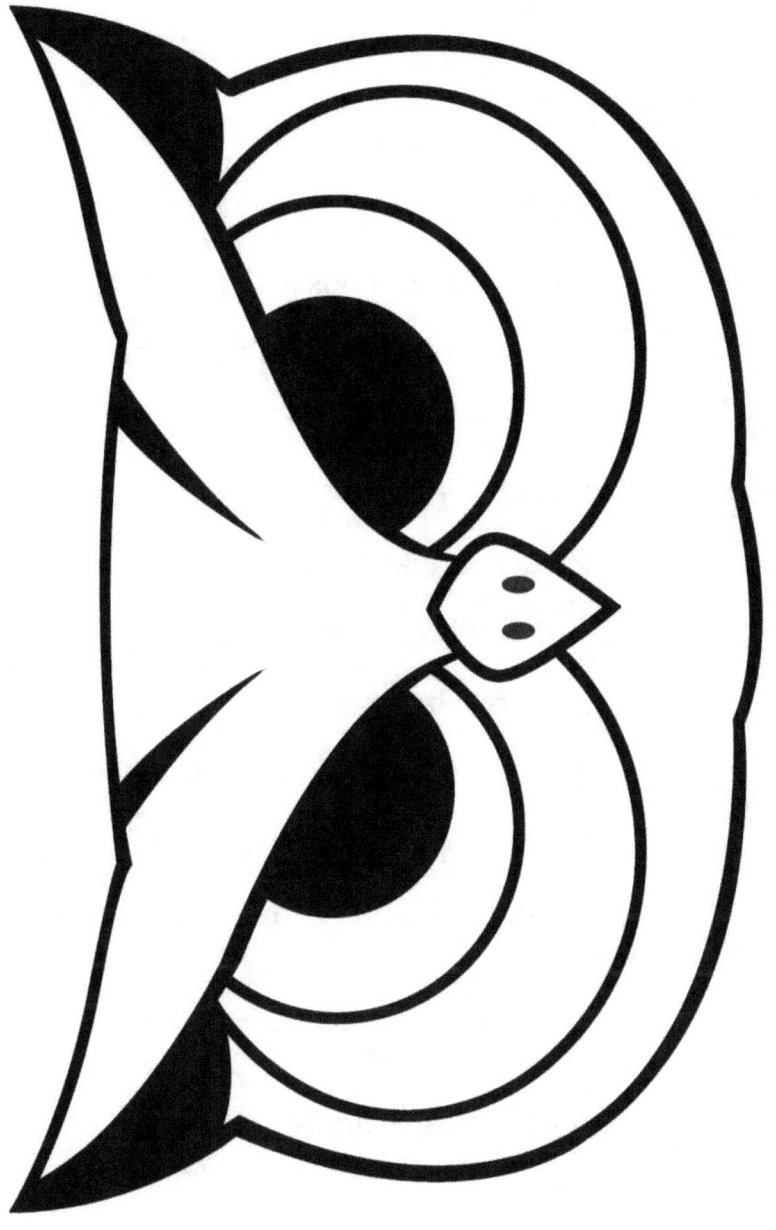

BOODY OWL

- Photocopy then paste on to stiff card
- Paint white and sprinkle with silver glitter
- Cut out the black eyes
- Punch out the black circles and loop rubber bands through them to hold on the ears

Vocabulary in Chapter E²

1. **adjoining** — bordering
2. **ambiguous** — having several possible meanings
3. **chasm** — deep cleft in the earth's surface
4. **compromised** — not functioning properly
5. **condemn** — judge severely
6. **cower** — crouch in fear
7. **domination** — rule, sway or control
8. **equilibrium** — a state of balance
9. **esoteric** — secret; known only to a select few
10. **gist** — the main part of a matter
11. **hallucination** — an illusion or delusion of the mind
12. **hypothetical** — supposing
13. **incriminating** — accuse of a crime
14. **keening** — wail for the dead
15. **ordain** — decree
16. **skinchanger** — shapeshifter; creature with the ability to magically change its appearance
17. **steepled** — looking like a church spire
18. **thrall** — slave
19. **unrelenting** — refusing to change; merciless
20. **warped** — twisted
21. **zenith** — highest point

ORDER THE EVENTS

Order the events in Dallan's re-telling of his escape from the Court of the Snow Demons

1	Dallan was sheep-herding on the pasture near Wreathwatch Pass
2	Dallan became disoriented and started to freeze
3	The mist began to lift
4	Dallan went towards the castle
5	A snow-storm came up without warning
6	Dallan saw the turrets of a castle and thought he was hallucinating
7	Dallan stumbled through the blizzard and got lost
8	The Wreathwatch Woman went to save other lost travellers
9	Dallan put one foot after another and hoped not to fall in a drift
10	Dallan became the adoring thrall of the Wreathwatch Woman
11	Dallan heard a voice like a sigh from the centre of the storm
12	The Wreathwatch Woman fed off Dallan's anger and resentment
13	The Wreathwatch Woman called curses down from the sky
14	Dallan ran out into the storm, taking the Helmet
15	Dallan lost his sight from the bitterly cold snow
16	Dallan ran into Madmerry's cottage
17	Wolves and snow-leopards were sent after Dallan
18	Madmerry helped Dallan onto a horse so they both escaped
19	The Wreathwatch Woman promised Dallan his heart's desire
20	Dallan looked for a sheepfold and its hut

Read the description of the Wreathwatch Pass and fill in the landscape around the Court of the Snow Demons below.

Vocabulary in Chapter F²

1. **annihilation** — destruction
2. **centripetal** — a force always directed towards the centre of a path
3. **mage** — magician
4. **potential** — possible, not actual
5. **replicate** — repeat or duplicate
6. **rival** — opponent
7. **siphon** — convey water through a tube

Hector has some memorable lines during the story. Pick your favourite quote so far and write it in the speech bubble. Draw in the cuffs around his ankles.

Vocabulary in Chapter G²

1.	**encroaching**	to advance beyond proper limits
2.	**famine**	extreme hunger
3.	**feign**	pretend deceptively
4.	**fretfully**	irritably
5.	**gladiator**	prizefighter, usually with a sword
6.	**inexorably**	unyielding
7.	**lattice**	a structure of crossed strips of wood or metal forming a diamond pattern
8.	**manifestly**	obviously
9.	**petty**	of little importance
10.	**puckered**	wrinkled
11.	**slewed**	twisted sideways
12.	**temporal**	enduring for a comparatively short time
13.	**unbridled**	not controlled

Assonance: *words that sound alike*

The words *letters*, *lattice* and *lettuce* are assonances. Identify each correctly.

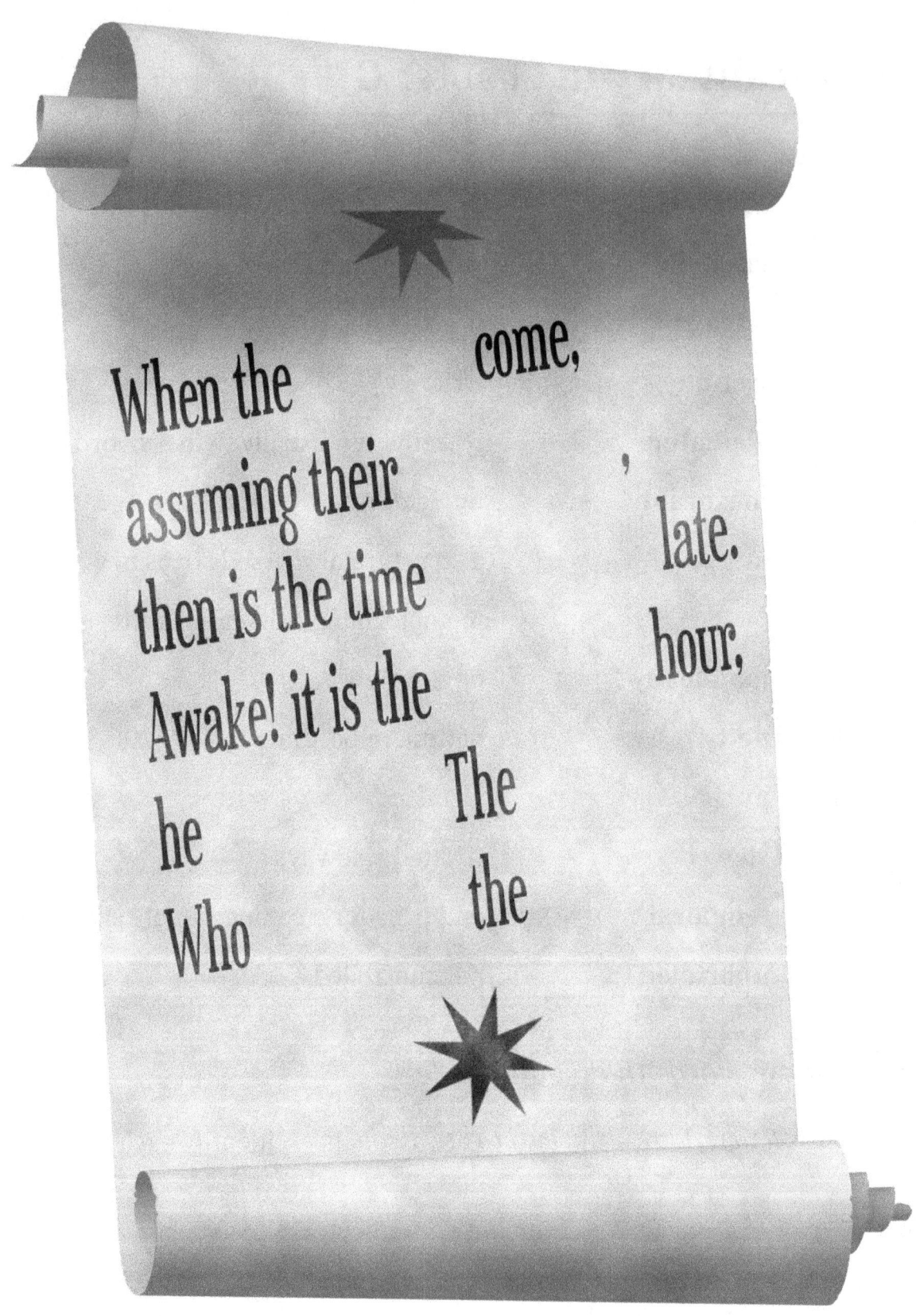

Fill in the missing words in the prophecy scroll about the coming of the Days.

Be Thou My Vision

Ancient Irish poem, ca. 8th cent.
Tr. by Mary E. Byrne 1905, Versified by Eleanor H. Hull 1912
Traditional Irish melody
Arr. by David Evans, 1927
Hymn Tune: SLANE

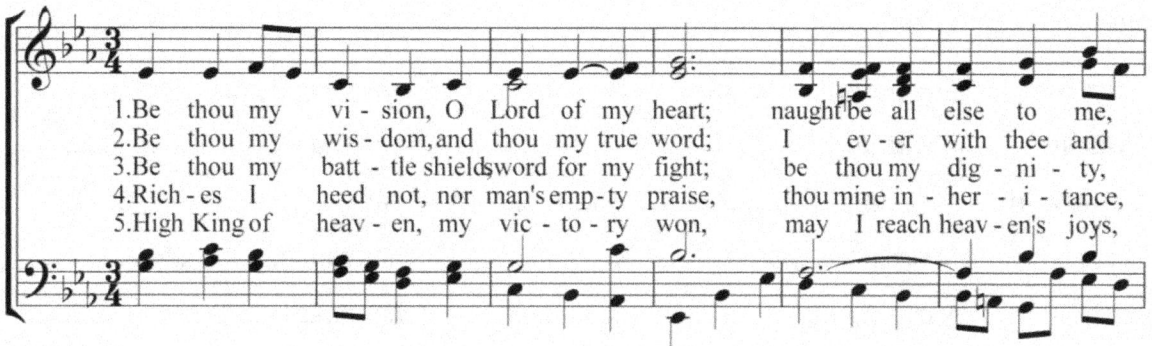

1. Be thou my vi-sion, O Lord of my heart; naught be all else to me,
2. Be thou my wis-dom, and thou my true word; I ev-er with thee and
3. Be thou my batt-tle shield, sword for my fight; be thou my dig-ni-ty,
4. Rich-es I heed not, nor man's emp-ty praise, thou mine in-her-i-tance,
5. High King of heav-en, my vic-to-ry won, may I reach heav-en's joys,

save that thou art. thou my best thought by day or by
thou with me, Lord; thou my great Fa-ther, I thy true
thou my de-light, thou my soul's shel-ter, thou my high
now and al-ways: thou and thou on-ly first in my
O bright heav'n's Sun! Heart of my own heart, what-ev-er be-

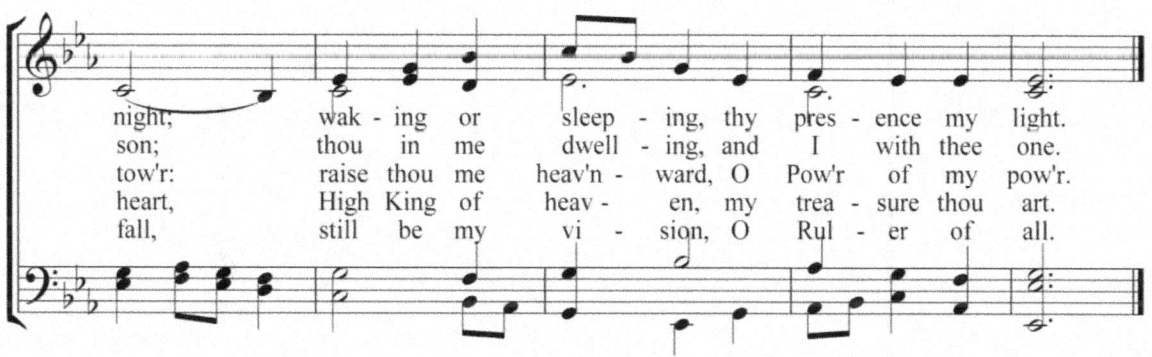

night; wak-ing or sleep-ing, thy pres-ence my light.
son; thou in me dwell-ing, and I with thee one.
tow'r: raise thou me heav'n-ward, O Pow'r of my pow'r.
heart, High King of heav-en, my trea-sure thou art.
fall, still be my vi-sion, O Rul-er of all.

Choosing **Names** 5

The names of the seven main characters in *Daystar* are very carefully chosen to reflect something about their personality and their nature. For instance, Emyr is Welsh for *honour*.

Using books about names or the internet, see if you can discover the meaning for the following names and what language they come from. Some may be very difficult to find. Some may have more than one meaning.

Ancelin	Meaning:..	Language: ....
Boudicca	Meaning:..	Language: ....
Cindurrah	Meaning:..	Language: ....
Dallan	Meaning:..	Language: ....
Ector	Meaning:..	Language: ....
Fern	Meaning:..	Language: ....
Ginevra	Meaning:..	Language: ....

Choose one of the characters above (or another from the story whose name you have researched) and design a coat-of-arms to go with the character's name.

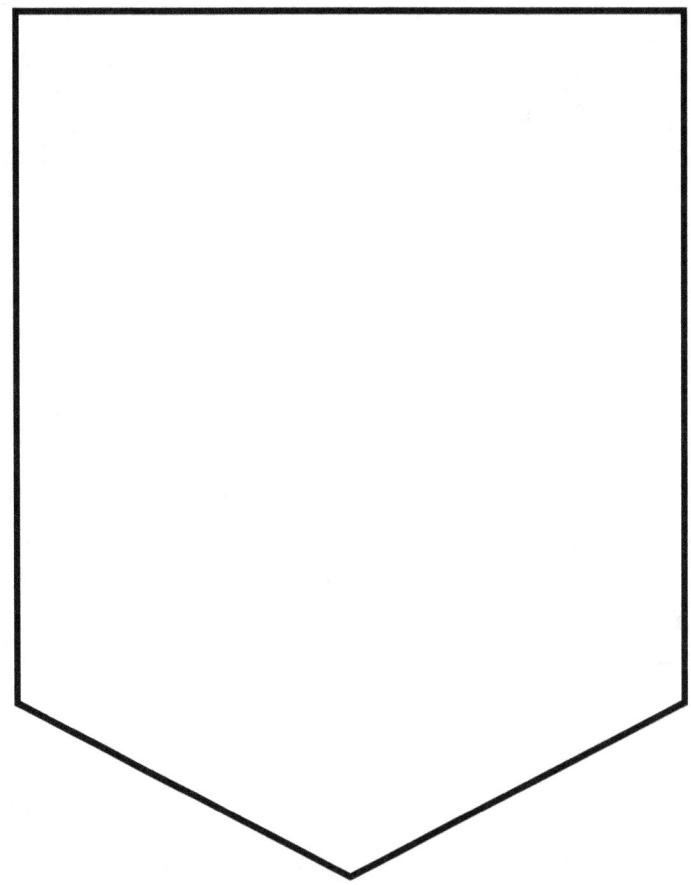

Design a coat–of–arms for yourself that reflects the meaning of your own name. If your name has an unknown meaning, design it following your final choice in *Choosing Names 1*.

- Choose a motto for yourself.
- Include drawings of the things you love—a book for reading; skateboard for skating and so on.
- Coats–of–arms sometimes feature animals. Draw your favourite animal on the outside, holding something up.

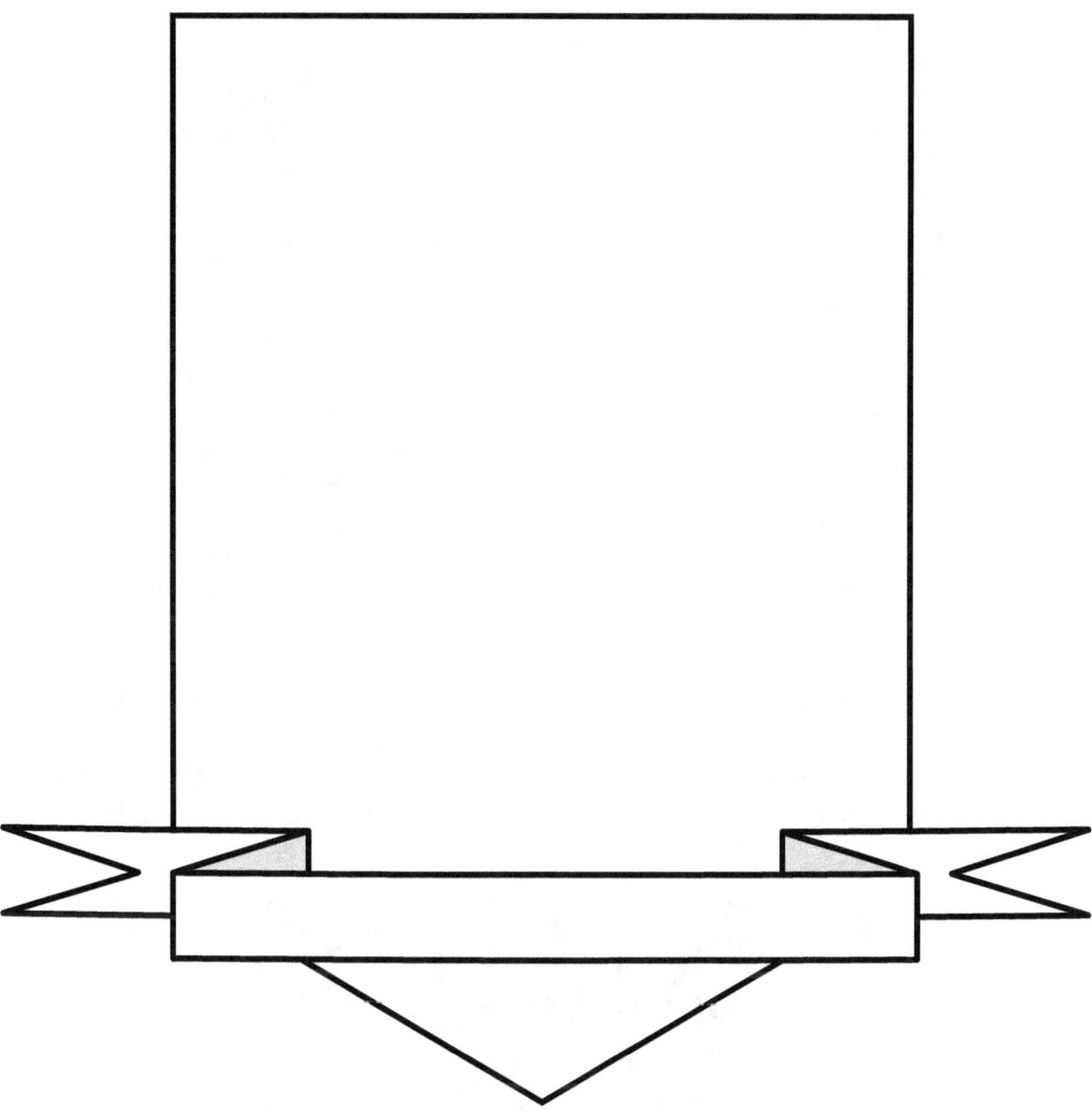

Research the national coat-of-arms and the coat-of-arms for your state.

What do they represent? _____

Why do we have them? _____

WHO'S WHO IN AUBERON AND BEYOND

(1) Who is the king of Auberon?
    (a) Maurtz
    (b) Rogin
    (c) Gratian
    (d) Barbizca

(2) Who is the king of Fyrzentsou?
    (a) Maurtz
    (b) Rogin
    (c) Gratian
    (d) Barbizca

(3) Who is the captain of the King's Shield?
    (a) Maurtz
    (b) Rogin
    (c) Gratian
    (d) Barbizca

(4) Who is the queen of Auberon?
    (a) Maurtz
    (b) Rogin
    (c) Gratian
    (d) Barbizca

(5) What is Mintaka?
    (a) A finch
    (b) A peacock
    (c) A chicken
    (d) A horse

(6) What is Rigel?
    (a) A finch
    (b) A peacock
    (c) A chicken
    (d) A horse

(7) What is Harrowfell?
    (a) A cliff
    (b) A castle
    (c) A swamp
    (d) A country

(8) What is Vircontium?
    (a) A cliff
    (b) A castle
    (c) A swamp
    (d) A country

(9) What is Auberon?
    (a) A cliff
    (b) A castle
    (c) A swamp
    (d) A country

(10) Who is Tybold?
    (a) Crown prince of Auberon
    (b) Ansey's step-brother
    (c) Captain of the King's Shield
    (d) One of Ansey's tutors

Choosing **Names** 6

- How many seven letter names can you find?

☐ Ancelin   ☐ Emyr   ☐ Madmerry

☐ Boody   ☐ Fern   ☐ Mintaka

☐ Candle   ☐ Freutim   ☐ Rigel

☐ Cindurrah   ☐ Hector   ☐ The Song

☐ Dallan   ☐ Ginevra   ☐ Uller

☐ Daystar   ☐ Gratian   ☐ Ysanne

Internet research

Which of the following names **don't** have to do with the *morning star*? After each name, write what language it comes from.

- Arousyag
- Ayelet
- Bellatrix
- Danika
- Éarendel

- Fetuao
- Gwendydd
- Heylel
- Jesus
- Keiyona

- Kōpū
- Lucifer
- Sitara
- Tariq
- Zornitsa

Find another 3 names that mean *morning star* or *daystar*.

- _____
- _____
- _____

Dodecahedron

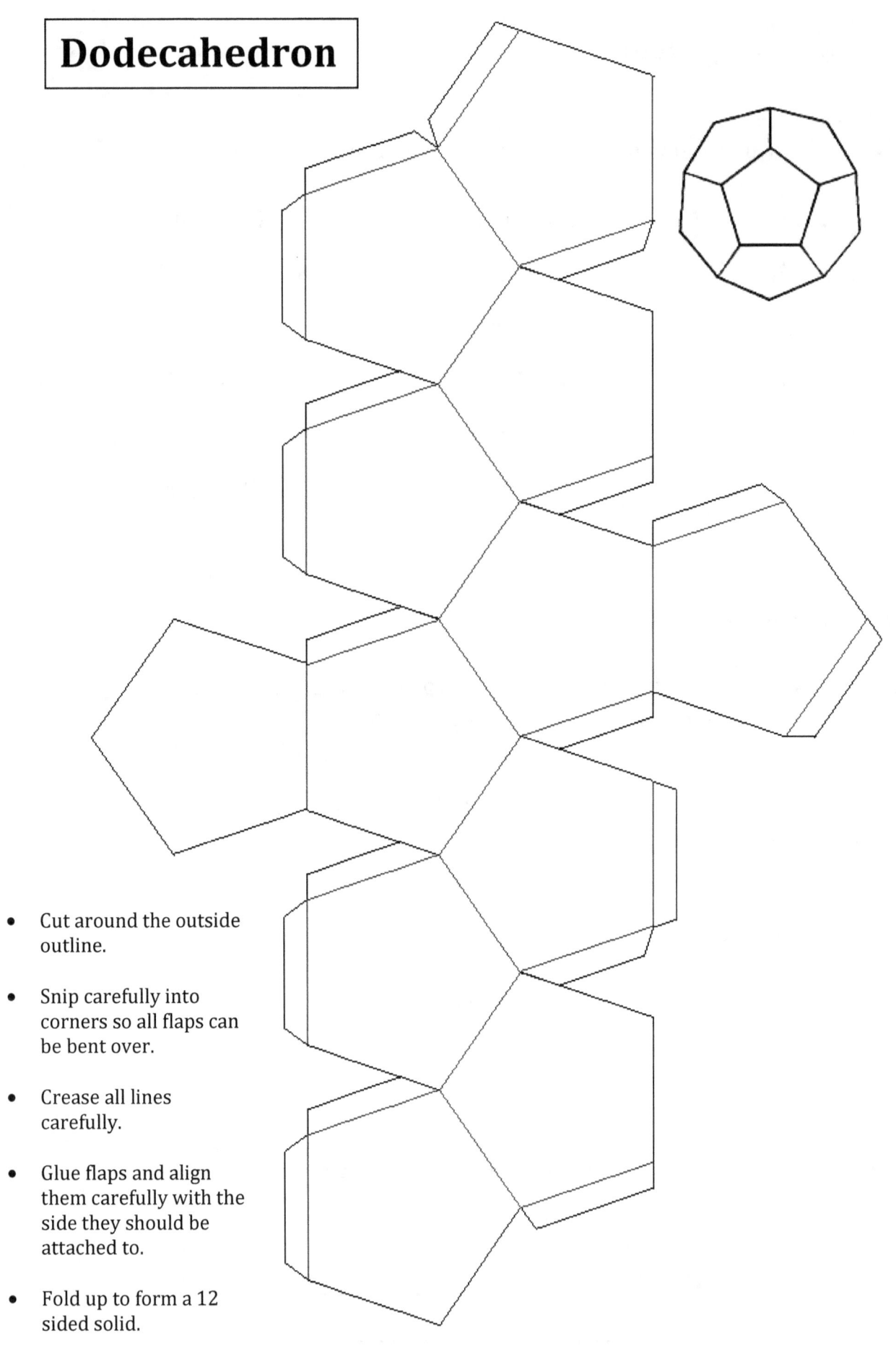

- Cut around the outside outline.

- Snip carefully into corners so all flaps can be bent over.

- Crease all lines carefully.

- Glue flaps and align them carefully with the side they should be attached to.

- Fold up to form a 12 sided solid.

Vocabulary in Chapter A³

1.	**adamant**	utterly unyielding
2.	**congealed**	change from a soft state to a harder one
3.	**converge**	tend towards a meeting point
4.	**dawdle**	move slowly
5.	**dispatch**	send off with speed
6.	**gruesome**	causing horror
7.	**nonplussed**	puzzled completely
8.	**slavering**	slobber; drool
9.	**sublime**	high in thought
10.	**ululate**	howl like a wolf
11.	**unanimous**	in complete agreement
12.	**vigilance**	state of being watchful

Water inside water

A glacier is like a frozen river. An englacial stream is therefore like a river inside a river.

Can you think of any other situations where water flows inside water? What are they?

_____
_____
_____
_____

Naming Days 1

Each of the main characters in *Daystar* corresponds to a day of the week. An old rhyme was thought to tell the fortunes of newborn children by the day on which they were born:

> *Monday's child is fair of face,*
> *Tuesday's child is full of grace,*
> *Wednesday's child is full of woe,*
> *Thursday's child has far to go,*
> *Friday's child is loving and giving,*
> *Saturday's child works hard for a living,*
> *And the child that is born on the Sabbath day*
> *Is bonny and blithe, and good and gay.*

1. What does 'Sabbath' mean?..

2. What does 'gay' mean in its original, older sense?...

3. Why is Sunday called the 'Sabbath Day' in this rhyme?

   ....

4. In *Daystar*, Sunday is the first weekday. What then is the Sabbath in the story?

   ....

5. Match each of the Seven Days in the story to the character:

Sunday's Child	Ansey
Monday's Child	Boody
Tuesday's Child	Dallan
Wednesday's Child	Fern
Thursday's Child	Ginevra
Friday's Child	Hector
Saturday's Child	Madmerry

6. Do any of them fit the fortune told for them in the rhyme? If so, which ones?

   ....

7. What day were you born?

   ....

   (You can find out using Zeller's Algorithm at
   http://www.mathsisfun.com/games/dayofweek.html)

   Check this using an Excel 2007 spreadsheet as follows:

   Point to Consider before you start

   Make sure you know the date format used on your computer. This sets the order of the day and month. For example, 05/11/2011 can be read by your computer as either 11 May or 5 November depending on the date format setting.

   (a)   Type your birth date using the short date format (such as 07/12/02) into a cell on a worksheet.

   (b)   Press the **ENTER** key on the keyboard.

   (c)   Now click on the cell in which you've typed your birth date to make it the active cell.

   (d)   Click on the *Home* tab.

   (e)   Click on the down arrow beside the *Number Format* button on the ribbon to open the drop down menu.

   (f)   Click on **Long Date** in the menu to change the format of the active cell to the long date format. This will include the day of the week.

   (g)   Look back at the cell containing your birth date. It should now include the day of the week on which you were born.

   Based on:
   http://spreadsheets.about.com/od/spreadsheetlessonplans/qt/090727-on-what-day-was--i-born.htm
   (Ted French)

8. There are many parodies of *Monday's Child*. Find out what a parody is and write a rhyme of your own to suit yourself and your friends.

   ....
   ....
   ....
   ....
   ....
   ....

Vocabulary in Chapter B³

1.	**budge**	move slightly or begin to move
2.	**culinary**	to do with cooking
3.	**dissipate**	scatter in different directions
4.	**embankment**	a bank raised to hold back water
5.	**entrails**	internal parts
6.	**gossamer**	having the texture of fine, filmy cobweb
7.	**immune**	protected from disease
8.	**obtuse**	not quick to understand
9.	**rapturously**	full of a feeling of delight
10.	**reconnoitre**	inspect an enemy's position
11.	**reconstitute**	reconstruct
12.	**seduction**	act of tempting
13.	**shale**	a clay-like rock
14.	**swathe**	wrap, bind or swaddle
15.	**wince**	tense the body
16.	**writhing**	twisting about

Book Link

from Many-Coloured Realm

'And now that I've got a moonchild, too,' Chris almost wailed, 'what am I going to do with it?'

'That's up to you, of course,' Artemys said, 'but most folk who asked for an audience were hoping for three wishes.'

'What wishes?'

'Anything,' Artemys said. 'Anything your heart can desire or your mind can conceive. That is what the moonchild can give you.'

'Wow!' Robby said.

'Deep trouble,' said Chris, with a look of horror.

'It becomes even more apparent to me with every passing minute why the moonchild chose you,' Artemys said. 'You're right. It is not something to rejoice in. Sensible people would avoid the responsibility. Thoughtless wishes are almost always disastrous. Even good ones. There was a king, centuries ago, whose wish was for his people never to be hungry again. They weren't. Because they all died that same day. And long before that, there was the countess, Solveigra, who desired to live forever. She does, but without eternal youth, it is a torment to her.'

'Oh,' Robby said, looking at Chris. 'I'm glad it's you and not me.'

He grimaced at her. Then he turned back to Artemys. 'Do you think it would be all right if I wish for Stephen to be free?'

Artemys was thoughtful. 'It might be,' he said.

(a) Which character appears in both *Many-Coloured Realm* & *Daystar*?

(b) What other name does she go by?

(c) What was her wish?

(d) What did she forget to include in her wish?

(e) What do we learn in *Daystar* is her weakness?

(f) What is the other name for the Airbridge of the Osiirins? Draw it in the picture on the previous page.

Naming **Days** 2

'No one expects the days to be gods.' Ralph Waldo Emerson

Where do the names of the weekdays come from? See if you can match the name of the day to its origin.

Sunday is named after	The **moon**, which in olden times was considered to be a planet
Monday is named after	The Anglo–Saxon god, **Woden**, equivalent to Norse Odin and the Roman messenger god, Mercury
Tuesday is named after	The god **Saturn** who was father of Jupiter, the ruler of the Roman gods
Wednesday is named after	The Anglo–Saxon god, **Tiw**, who was the arbiter of single combats and equivalent to Roman Mars
Thursday is named after	The **sun**, which in olden times was considered to be a planet
Friday is named after	The Norse god **Thor** who like the Roman Jupiter had a thunder hammer and wielded lightning
Saturday is named after	The Norse goddess **Freyja** who was the equivalent of the Roman Venus

Research:

English	**French**	**German**	Your choice
Sunday			
Monday			
Tuesday			
Wednesday			
Thursday			
Friday			
Saturday			

Have you noticed a connection between the names of the days of the weekdays and the planets of the solar system? It's not so obvious in English, but if you look closely at the French, you might be able to spot the pattern.

Circle any of the following which have a corresponding day of the week:

Mercury, Venus, Earth, Mars, Jupiter, Saturn, Uranus, Neptune

Vocabulary in Chapter C³

1. **alpine** — used to describe flowers or grasses growing on mountains above the tree limit
2. **bleached** — to remove colour
3. **cairn** — a heap of stones set up as a landmark
4. **crevasse** — a deep rift in glacial ice or in the ground
5. **fealty** — faithfulness to a lord or master
6. **fissure** — narrow opening
7. **jinx** — a person or thing said to bring bad luck
8. **loll** — lean in a lazy way
9. **lope** — run with a long, easy stride
10. **penalty** — punishment for breaking a law or rule
11. **prescribe** — set down a rule
12. **shin** — front part of the leg from knee to ankle
13. **superstition** — a belief that events, such as seeing a black cat, are omens that evil things are about to happen
14. **upfells** — upper fells, that is, high mountainsides above the alpine tree line

Choosing **Names** 7
Meanings

- What is your name? [ ]

- What does it mean? [ ]

Different sources will often give different answers for the meaning of names. So check out at least two different books or websites for the meaning and cite your source. Some comprehensive websites include:
http://www.20000-names.com/index.htm and
http://www.behindthename.com/
There are also many good books you can consult, such as:
The Great Australian and New Zealand Book of Baby Names
Names from Here and Far: The New Holland Dictionary of Names

- Choose one of your favourite characters from *The Days Are Numbered*. Write down the name, its meaning and the source of your information.

[ ]

- Can you find another name with the same general meaning? Write it down here.

[ ]

- Can you find another name with the same general meaning as your own? Write it down here.

[ ]

- If you could change your name, would you?

[ ]

- If you wouldn't change your name, explain why you like it.

[ ]

- If you would change your name, what would you change it to and why?

[ ]

Vocabulary in Chapter D³

1. **aggressive** — menacing; makes unprovoked attacks
2. **cirque** — bowl-shaped, steep-walled basin on a mountain carved by glaciation
3. **contemptuous** — scornful or disrespectful
4. **eddy** — a whirling motion in a stream
5. **nonchalant** — coolly unconcerned
6. **retrieve** — recover or regain
7. **saunter** — stroll
8. **threshold** — entrance to a house or building.
9. **trespass** — wrongful entry
10. **wraith** — ghost or spirit

Draw an arrow to either of the two cirques in the photograph of the glacier on the left.

The Bowl of the Field of Stars

All of the following words describe a landscape feature like a *cirque*. Match each of the words to its correct meaning and also research which language the word comes from.

Language	**Word for** *bowl in the landscape*	**Meaning**
	Cirque	Mortar Grinder
	Corrie	Valley
	Cwm	Arena
	Makhtesh	Pot *or* Cauldron

There are only four cirques in Australia. What are their names?

- _____
- _____
- _____
- _____

Vocabulary in Chapter E³

1.	**advent**	coming or arriving
2.	**alabaster**	a translucent stone, usually white
3.	**amethyst**	purple gemstone
4.	**anti-climax**	event that is far less important than expected
5.	**brocade**	fabric woven with elaborate design
6.	**calibre**	degree of excellence
7.	**cataclysm**	disaster
8.	**cloth-of-gold**	cloth woven with silk threads interspersed with gold
9.	**colossal**	huge, gigantic
10.	**crestfallen**	discouraged
11.	**dissension**	argument causing division
12.	**emperor**	ruler over an empire
13.	**extinct**	no longer in existence
14.	**frostbite**	injury caused by extreme cold
15.	**gawking**	staring stupidly
16.	**intermission**	short interval between events
17.	**iridescent**	displaying many lustrous colours
18.	**melodrama**	a play or act in which emotions are exaggerated

19.	**millennium**	thousand years
20.	**moraine**	a ridge of boulders, gravel, sand or clay dumped by a glacier
21.	**nonplussed**	puzzled completely
22.	**obituary**	notice of a person's death
23.	**over-compensation**	a pronounced striving to conceal a character trait
24.	**pedantic**	overly concerned with small details
25.	**quartz**	one of the most common minerals; a glass-like rock crystal
26.	**rose quartz**	a pale pink glass-like rock crystal
27.	**sibyl**	a female prophet
28.	**soothsayer**	a person who foretells the future
29.	**stalactites**	a deposit, shaped like an icicle, which hangs from the roof of a cave
30.	**translucent**	diffusing light, like frosted glass
31.	**vomitorium**	passage in an ancient theatre leading to the seats (the passage was considered to 'vomit' out spectators); mistakenly thought to be a room where Roman diners deliberately threw up between banquet courses to make room for more food

GROUNDED!

Research, if necessary, to match these geological items:

Stalactite	A flow of meltwater inside a glacier
Stalagmite	A deep crack in rock
Englacial Stream	A rock formation that rises from the floor of a cave and is composed of deposits from ceiling drippings
Rose Quartz	A rock formation that hangs from the ceiling of caves
Amethyst	A deep crack in an ice sheet or glacier
Crevasse	A form of quartz that has a purplish or lilac colouring
Crevice	A semi-precious gemstone like glass with a pale pink to rosy red colouring
Avalanche	A bowl-shaped valley at the head of a glacier
Cirque	A large body of dense ice moving extremely slowly downhill under its own weight
Glacier	Snowslide or snowslip; a rapid fall of snow down a slope

WonderWord 10

TITLE: **In the** _ _ _ _ _ _ _

Chapter E³ ~ Level: *medium*

Directions for words could be any of ⇒ ⇐ ⇑ ⇓ ↗ ↘ ↗ ↙

T	U	E	N	G	L	A	C	I	A	L	S
H	C	T	A	W	H	T	A	E	R	W	T
K	R	A	E	C	H	O	E	S	N	A	R
R	Y	N	U	Q	U	A	R	T	Z	Y	E
A	S	I	C	E	S	T	E	P	S	E	A
D	T	F	U	R	S	G	E	M	S	L	M
C	A	R	V	I	N	G	S	G	L	O	W
E	L	T	N	E	G	E	L	T	B	U	S
U	N	D	E	R	G	R	O	U	N	D	!

Find the following words:

- Englacial
- Stream
- Wreathwatch
- Way
- Crystal
- Underground
- Echoes
- Ice steps
- Carvings
- Subtle Gentle
- Quartz
- Furs
- Gems
- Dark
- Glow
- Cap

The leftover letters complete the title.

Choosing **Names** 8

Nicknames

Many of the characters in the story have nicknames or even pseudonyms 'false names' (a bit like a 'tag') to disguise who they really are.

In the following list, choose which of the following applies: real name, nickname or pseudonym. If you're unsure, you can consult the Index at the back of the book. If it's a nickname or a pseudonym, write down the real name of the person.

1. Ancelin ....
2. Ansey ....
3. Boody ....
4. Boudicca's Chariot ....
5. Boy Wonder ....
6. Cindurrah ....
7. Dallan ....
8. Ector ....
9. Emyr ....
10. Fern ....
11. Ginevra ....
12. Hector ....
13. Madmerry ....
14. Merry ....

What is a nickname? ....

Some people give nicknames to others to be friendly and some do it to be offensive. What actions can you take if someone tries to bully you with an offensive nickname?

....

....

Vocabulary in Chapter F³

1.	**camouflage**	disguise in order to deceive an enemy
2.	**concede**	admit that something is good or right
3.	**contingent**	conditional
4.	**counterpane**	bedspread
5.	**fulsome**	excessive or overdone
6.	**grotesque**	odd or unnatural in appearance
7.	**junction**	place of joining
8.	**meander**	wind around or take an indirect course
9.	**mellifluous**	sweet or smoothly flowing
10.	**radial**	arranged like rays
11.	**scoundrel**	villain
12.	**slag**	waste left over from sorting coal

Vocabulary in Chapter G³

1.	**abyss**	a deep, immeasurable chasm
2.	**accost**	confront boldly
3.	**benediction**	blessing
4.	**brawn**	muscular strength

5.	**chivalry**	ideal qualifications of a knight, including courtesy, generosity, bravery and fighting skill
6.	**delegation**	group chosen to represent a wider body of people
7.	**derision**	ridicule or mockery
8.	**greaves**	armour for the legs
9.	**hypostatic**	placed under to give support
10.	**impregnable**	strong enough to withstand all attacks
11.	**pannier**	basket for carrying goods
12.	**portcullis**	a strong grating to prevent passage at a gateway
13.	**pseudolithic**	false rock
14.	**psychological**	of the mind
15.	**pukesome**	giving a feeling of wanting to throw up
16.	**sentinel**	watching guard
17.	**solemnity**	earnest or serious
18.	**surfeit**	excess; too much
19.	**surveillance**	watch kept over a suspect or prisoner
20.	**tectonic**	of the earth's crust
21.	**titanic**	gigantic; huge
22.	**tykes**	children
23.	**unabashed**	not ashamed or uncertain
24.	**visor**	moveable part of a helmet with eye-slits
25.	**vitreous**	glassy

WonderWord 11

Chapter A⁴ and B⁴ ~ Level: *easy* → *medium*

Directions for words could be any of ⇒ ⇐ ⇑ ⇓ ↗ ↘ ↗ ↖

R	H	O	D	R	I	H	A	R	K	E	L
L	T	H	E	Q	N	E	I	L	O	X	O
A	A	F	O	L	I	T	T	G	X	E	R
L	P	D	S	Q	N	N	O	R	E	R	D
L	A	P	Y	U	U	E	B	A	N	X	A
Y	T	E	A	Y	M	M	I	T	O	E	N
A	R	R	D	S	S	R	A	I	P	S	C
N	I	C	E	T	K	A	S	A	H	D	E
D	C	I	H	E	O	P	N	N	O	R	L
V	U	V	T	I	F	Y	S	N	N	A	I
A	S	A	G	N	O	B	B	L	E	U	N
N	E	L	B	B	O	W	A	R	D	G	E

The leftover letters form the the title.

- Rhodri Harke
- Lady Ysanne
- The Q
- Gratian
- Wobble
- Lord Ancelin
- Xerxes
- Xenophon
- Patricus
- Percival
- Parment
- Guards
- Munin
- Quystein
- Tobias
- Olien
- The Days
- Lally and Van
- Nobble

Vocabulary in Chapter A⁴

1. **antiquated** — no longer used; old-fashioned
2. **aptitude** — special talent
3. **conglomeration** — a mass that sticks together; a cluster
4. **cyclops** — a giant monster with a single eye in its forehead
5. **dishevelled** — untidy or disordered
6. **diversification** — manufacturing a variety of products
7. **elves** — fairy-like beings thought to have magical powers
8. **hypocrite** — person who pretends to have virtues or beliefs but does not really possess them
9. **implacable** — cannot be pacified
10. **infantile** — immature or weak
11. **lucrative** — profitable or money-making
12. **luminous** — radiating or reflecting light
13. **mercenaries** — professional soldiers hired to serve in a foreign army
14. **merchandise** — goods in a store
15. **morality** — keeping the rules of right conduct
16. **perishable** — subject to decay
17. **puerile** — childishly foolish

18. **recruit** — new member of a group (especially armed forces)

19. **rummage** — search thoroughly

20. **sprite** — like an elf, fairy or goblin

21. **sustenance** — means of nourishing or sustaining life

22. **wizened** — withered or shriveled

Project:

William Wilberforce is famous for his lifetime of work towards the abolition of slavery. Although there are still millions of slaves in the world today, Wilberforce is justly famous because he changed the views of society. Before his time, ordinary people thought it was ok to own slaves; after his work, they did not. He was also concerned for the treatment of animals and was instrumental in setting up the RSPCA.

Choose one of the following:

(1) Watch the film *Amazing Grace* and write a film review of at least 200 words.

(2) Research the work of the RSPCA and interview someone who works there. Write up the interview (at least 200 words).

(3) Find out what organisations work today to abolish slavery. Choose one of them and write 200 words about their work and deliver your findings as a short speech to the class.

(4) Make a poster about William Wilberforce or John Newton who changed from being a slave trader to an abolitionist.

(5) Ask your principal for a special 'mufti' day at school to collect money to help one organisation trying to help slaves.

Vocabulary in Chapter B⁴

1.	**absorption**	uptake of substance into another material, such as water into a cloth
2.	**chiselling**	working with a wedge-like tool to cut stone or wood
3.	**condone**	overlook or pardon
4.	**despondent**	feeling of hopelessness
5.	**emaciated**	thin and wasted
6.	**integrity**	honesty and soundness of character
7.	**interminable**	unending
8.	**livid**	furiously angry
9.	**makeshift**	temporary substitute
10.	**massacre**	unnecessary killing of a large number of human beings
11.	**miffed**	put in an irritable mood
12.	**omnipotence**	possessing unlimited power
13.	**omniscience**	possessing unlimited knowledge
14.	**pompous**	overly dignified or high-flown
15.	**rime**	coating of ice particles caused by water droplets freezing on contact with a cold object
16.	**rivulets**	small streams
17.	**rout**	disorderly flight in retreat from battle

18.	**thaw**	melt
19.	**toga**	loose outer garment worn by Roman citizens
20.	**unchancy**	unlucky and dangerous

Vocabulary in Chapter C⁴

1.	**acute**	intense
2.	**ancestry**	family line
3.	**billets**	lodging for soldiers
4.	**briefed**	given an outline or summary
5.	**camaraderie**	friendship
6.	**deficiency**	shortage or inadequacy
7.	**effreets**	evil demons (also spelled afreets)
8.	**envoy**	messenger
9.	**fluently**	spoken or written with ease
10.	**foully**	gross and offensive
11.	**gauntlet**	metal glove
12.	**inadvertedly**	mistakenly or accidentally
13.	**insignificance**	of little account
14.	**magnanimously**	extremely generously
15.	**mara-mares**	spirits of nightmare
16.	**perspective**	viewpoint
17.	**quizzical**	odd or comical

18. **remorse** — deep regret for wrongdoing
19. **sufficient** — enough
20. **stricken** — affected by a wound, fear or trouble
21. **tousling** — disordering
22. **troll** — evil-tempered race of giants from the folklore of Northern Europe

Sun, Moon & Stars

In the world of Auberon–Zamberg, the sun is a fireflower with petals that open and close.

Draw the moon of Auberon–Zamberg in the space below and explain how it differs from Earth's moon.

What do the stars of Auberon–Zamberg look like?

_____
_____
_____

HECTOR FOX MASK ~

- Photocopy
- Paste on to stiff card
- Paint white and sprinkle with silver glitter
- Glue on whiskers
- Cut out the black eyes
- Punch out circles and loop rubber bands through them to hold on the ears

Vocabulary in Chapter D⁴

1. **alliance** — agreement to cooperate for a purpose
2. **appease** — satisfy to bring to a state of peace
3. **brethren** — persons from the same kinship group
4. **delegate** — person appointed to act for another
5. **endgame** — the final moves of any activity (but especially a game of chess)
6. **epitome** — a person or thing possessing a quality that makes it highest in its class
7. **implication** — suggestion from which a natural understanding is to be taken
8. **irony** — a statement that indicates the very opposite of the words expressed
9. **liege** — lord or king entitled to service
10. **negotiation** — discussion to arrange an agreement
11. **parley** — informal conference during a truce
12. **primeval** — ancient, from the first age
13. **savour** — delight in the taste
14. **squint** — look with eyes partly closed
15. **stealth** — secret procedure
16. **subterfuge** — artful way of avoiding a rule or consequence
17. **transpire** — occur; happen

ORDER THE EVENTS 5

Order the events which occur from the time the Days leave Mistmurk Height to the time they arrive in Ysgarde and meet the guard.

1	The manticores are heard baying in the distance, so the Days are forced to flee Mistmurk Height.
2	The White Mother tries to take the Powers from the Days when they've crossed the Airbridge which she calls 'Solveigra's Stair'.
3	The Days flee across the upfells of Fyrzentsou, trying to escape the people who've come up the mountain.
4	Dallan collapses while talking to Fern about the state of the country of Fyrzentsou.
5	Candle gives gifts to each of the Days and orders a huge feast with many courses.
6	The Days are taken up the Wreathwatch Way through the englacial stream and into the Nardelf.
7	Emyr offers to play the game of fletch with Wobble and Nobble and proposes a wager.
8	The Days flee down to the Airbridge with Candle and Zippy; they are concerned if it will hold their weight.
9	Candle rallies the dwarves to help the Knights of Renown, saying that Seven Days do not make one week, they just are weak.
10	The Days take the lift from the Nardelf up to the top of the pass across from Ysgarde.
11	Fern, Ginevra and Madmerry begin singing to calm their nerves during the fight on the Airbridge.
12	Hector realises the importance of the Scented Stones and why the people of Fyrzentsou are sniffing rocks.
13	The Days and two dwarves walk across the Pass from the lookout on top of the Nardelf to Ysgarde.
14	Ansey passes on to Lord Ancelin a ring and a shield given to him by The Song.
15	The Days meet Uller on the Airbridge; he is going to kill them but decides not to after he learns which days they were born.
16	The Days are helped by a dwarf legion to reach the safety of the Bowl of the Field of Stars.
17	Dallan asks Ansey for a sword to fight the manticores and proves himself a master of swordsmanship.
18	Wobble introduces himself, the Days and Nobble to the guard on the gate at Ysgarde.

WonderWord 12

Chapter ~ Level: *medium*

Directions for words could be any of ⇒ ⇐ ⇑ ⇓ ↗ ↘ ↗ ↘

E	D	A	C	E	D	W	Y
M	O	N	D	A	Y	E	A
T	S	W	T	S	H	D	D
H	U	E	W	E	T	N	R
U	N	E	O	Y	N	E	U
R	D	K	S	A	O	S	T
S	A	P	R	D	M	D	A
D	Y	A	U	I	A	A	S
A	E	E	O	R	V	Y	E
Y	N	L	H	F	O	N	E

(1) *Find each of the days of the week.*
(2) *Find the words that complete these statements:*

- 60 minutes = 1 ....
- 7 days = 1 ....
- 4 weeks = 1 ....
- 52 weeks = 1 ....
- 1 fortnight = ... weeks
- 10 years = 1 ....
- 366 days = 1 .... year
- 60 seconds = ... minute

(3) *The leftover letters say something about a week.*

MUNIN *or* HUGINN RAVEN MASK

- Paste on to stiff card
- Paint white and sprinkle with red glitter, decorate with feathers
- Cut out the eyes
- Punch out small circles and loop rubber bands through them to hold on the ears

Playing with Ones
(1)

1

1 + 1 =

1 + 1 + 1 =

1 + 1 + 1 + 1 =

1 + 1 + 1 + 1 + 1 =

1 + 1 + 1 + 1 + 1 + 1 =

1 + 1 + 1 + 1 + 1 + 1 + 1 =

We learn to count so we don't have to keep on adding up ....

1 + 1 = ... lots of ones

1 + 1 + 1 = ... lots of ones

1 + 1 + 1 + 1 = ... lots of ones

1 + 1 + 1 + 1 + 1 = ... lots of ones

1 + 1 + 1 + 1 + 1 + 1 = ... lots of ones

1 + 1 + 1 + 1 + 1 + 1 + 1 = ... lots of ones

Multiplying is a lazy shortcut so we don't have to keep adding up ones.

1 + 1 = ... × 1

1 + 1 + 1 = ... × 1

1 + 1 + 1 + 1 = ... × 1

1 + 1 + 1 + 1 + 1 = ... × 1

1 + 1 + 1 + 1 + 1 + 1 = ... × 1

1 + 1 + 1 + 1 + 1 + 1 + 1 = ... × 1

11 + 11 + 11 + 11 + 11 + 11 + 11 + 11 + 11 + 11 + 11 = ... × 11 =

111 + 111 + 111 + 111 + 111 + 111 + 111 + 111 + 111 + 111 + 111 + 111 + 111 +
111 + 111 + 111 + 111 + 111 + 111 + 111 + 111 + 111 + 111 + 111 + 111 + 111 +
111 + 111 + 111 + 111 + 111 + 111 + 111 + 111 + 111 + 111 + 111 + 111 + 111 +
111 + 111 + 111 + 111 + 111 + 111 + 111 + 111 + 111 + 111 + 111 + 111 + 111 +
111 + 111 + 111 + 111 + 111 + 111 + 111 + 111 + 111 + 111 + 111 + 111 + 111 +
111 + 111 + 111 + 111 + 111 + 111 + 111 + 111 + 111 + 111 + 111 + 111 + 111 +
111 + 111 + 111 + 111 + 111 + 111 + 111 + 111 + 111 + 111 + 111 + 111 + 111 +
111 + 111 + 111 + 111 + 111 + 111 + 111 + 111 + 111 + 111 + 111 + 111 + 111 +
111 + 111 + 111 + 111 + 111 + 111 + 111 = ... × 111 =

How many lots of 11 would you have to add up if you wanted the answer to equal the same as 11 × 7?

How many lots of 11 would you have to add up if you wanted the answer to equal the same as 11 × 17?

How many lots of 11 would you have to add up if you wanted the answer to equal the same as 11 × 111?

How many lots of 111 would you have to add up if you wanted the answer to equal the same as 111 × 7?

How many lots of 111 would you have to add up if you wanted the answer to equal the same as 111 × 17?

How many lots of 111 would you have to add up if you wanted the answer to equal the same as 111 × 1111?

How many lots of 1111 would you have to add up if you wanted the answer to equal the same as 1111 × 1111?

How many lots of 11111 would you have to add up if you wanted the answer to equal the same as 1111 × 11111?

How many lots of 1111111 would you have to add up if you wanted the answer to equal the same as 1111111111 × 1111111?

Playing with Ones
(2)

$1 \times 9 + 2 = $ ....

$12 \times 9 + 3 = $ ....

$123 \times 9 + 4 = $ ....

Fill in the following according to the pattern:

$1234 \times 9 + 5 = $ ....

$12345 \times 9 + 6 = $ ....

$123456 \times 9 + 7 = $ ....

$1234567 \times 9 + 8 = $ ....

$12345678 \times 9 + 9 = $ ....

Does the pattern keep working for $123456789 \times 9 + 10$? Check it out!

Choosing **Names** 9:

AKA ~ Also Known As

Ansey   aka   A.................... B .... C...........

Boody   aka   B..................... C.............................

Madmerry   aka   C...................... aka   M............................

Dallan   aka   B................ W................ aka   E..............

Hector   aka   E................

Ginevra   aka   G....................-....................-....................

Candle   aka   L................ of the N....................................

Gratian   aka   L............ C..................... of Y................

Solveigra aka   W........................ W....................

Uller   aka   P.................... aka X.................... X....................

Quystein   aka   T............ Q..................

The Song aka   R................ aka   T............ A.................... of D................

Do you have a nickname? ....

Do you have a username you use on social media? ....

What's your AKA?..

Calling Cards and Business Cards

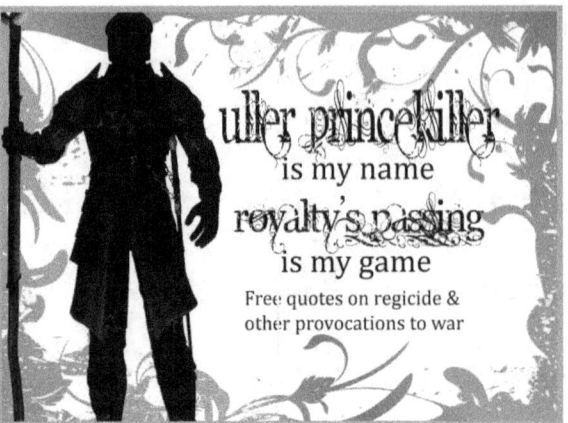

Create a calling card for one of the characters of *Daystar*. You can choose Hector or Uller again, if you like. Some other possibilities are below but you need not limit yourself to them. When you've made a calling card/business card for one of the characters, design one for yourself.

Xerxes Xenophon
Human Resource Manager
also specialising in Performing Elephants

Fawn of Dawn
Ginevra-'ayelet-hashachar
Address: White Tree, Auberon

Owl on the Prowl
Boudicca's Chariot
at your service
Address: White Tree, Auberon

Merry's Herbs
Madmerry and Dallan
Your trusted source for healing herbs
Address: White Canopy, Auberon

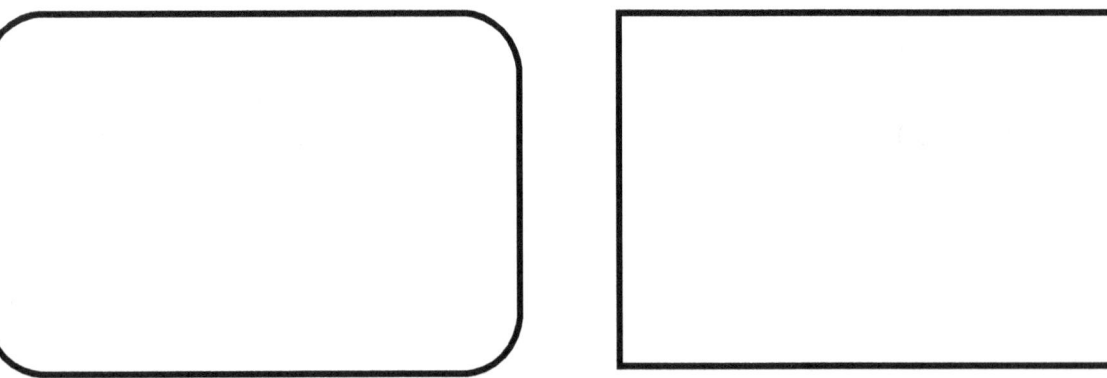

Playing with Ones
(3)

1 × 1 = ...

11 × 11 = ...

111 × 111 = ...

1111 × 1111 = ...

Use the pattern you've found to fill in the following (without calculating):

11111 × 11111 = ...

111111 × 111111 = ...

1111111 × 1111111 = ...

11111111 × 11111111 = ...

111111111 × 111111111 = ...

Does the pattern still hold for 1111111111 × 1111111111?
Check it out and write down the answer:

Playing with Ones
(4)

1 × 8 + 1 = ...

12 × 8 + 2 = ...

123 × 8 +3 = ...

Use the pattern you've discovered to fill in the following (without calculating):

1234 × 8 +4 = ...

12345 × 8 +5 = ...

123456 × 8 +6 = ...

1234567 × 8 +7= ....

12345678 × 8 +8 = ...

123456789 × 8 +9 = ...

Does the pattern still work for 1234567890 × 8 +10?

Check it out!

Playing with Ones
(5)

Counting numbers go up by ones. The value of a digit changes according to where it stands.

The value of the 1 in the following numbers changes as its position changes:
- 123
- 231
- 312

In the first instance, 1 is worth 100. In the second instance, it's worth 1 but in the third it's worth 10.

Millions	hundred thousands	ten thousands	thousands	Hundreds	tens	units

(1) In what place is the one in 10000 standing?

    (a) Millions
    (b) Hundred thousands
    (c) Ten thousands
    (d) Thousands
    (e) Hundreds

(2) In what place is the one in 100 standing?

    (a) Hundred thousands
    (b) Ten thousands
    (c) Thousands
    (d) Hundreds
    (e) Units

(3) In what place is the one in 1000000 standing?

    (a) Millions
    (b) Hundred thousands
    (c) Ten thousands
    (d) Hundreds
    (e) Units

(4) In what place is the one in 10 standing?

    (a) Millions
    (b) Thousands
    (c) Hundreds
    (d) Tens
    (e) Units

(5) In what place is the 3 in 300 standing?

    (a) Millions
    (b) Hundred thousands
    (c) Ten thousands
    (d) Thousands
    (e) Hundreds

(6) In what place is the 5 in 5000 standing?

    (a) Millions
    (b) Hundred thousands
    (c) Ten thousands
    (d) Thousands

Playing with Ones
(6)

10 + 1 = ...

100 + 1 = ...

1000 + 1 = ...

10000 + 1 = ...

100 + 10 = ...

1000 + 100 = ...

10000 + 1000 = ...

100000 + 10000 = ...

100 + 10 + 1 = ...

1000 + 100 + 10 = ...

10000 + 1000 + 100 = ...

100000 + 10000 + 1000 = ...

1000 + 100 + 10 + 1 = ...

10000 + 1000 + 100 + 10 = ...

100000 + 10000 + 1000 + 100 = ...

10000 + 1000 + 100 + 10 + 1 = ...

100000 + 10000 + 1000 + 100 + 10 = ...

100000 + 10000 + 1000 + 100 + 10 + 1 = ...

Playing with Ones
(7)

Powers

$1 \times 1 = 1$ to the power .... = $1^{...}$ =

$1 \times 1 \times 1 = 1$ to the power .... = $1^{...}$ =

$1 \times 1 \times 1 \times 1 = 1$ to the power .... = $1^{...}$ =

$1 \times 1 \times 1 \times 1 \times 1 = 1$ to the power .... = $1^{...}$ =

$1 \times 1 \times 1 \times 1 \times 1 \times 1 = 1$ to the power .... = $1^{...}$ =

$1 \times 1 \times 1 \times 1 \times 1 \times 1 \times 1 = 1$ to the power .... = $1^{...}$ =

$1 \times 1 \times 1 \times 1 \times 1 \times 1 \times 1 \times 1 = 1$ to the power .... = $1^{...}$ =

$1 \times 1 \times 1 \times 1 \times 1 \times 1 \times 1 \times 1 \times 1 = 1$ to the power .... = $1^{...}$ =

$1 \times 1 \times 1 \times 1 \times 1 \times 1 \times 1 \times 1 \times 1 \times 1 = 1$ to the power .... = $1^{...}$ =

$1 \times 1 \times 1 \times 1 \times 1 \times 1 \times 1 \times 1 \times 1 \times 1 \times 1 = 1$ to the power .... = $1^{...}$ =

$11 \times 11 = 11$ to the power .... = $11^{...}$ =

$11 \times 11 \times 11 = 11$ to the power .... = $11^{...}$ =

$11 \times 11 \times 11 \times 11 = 11$ to the power .... = $11^{...}$ =

How would you write:

11^1

11^0

Vocabulary in Chapter E⁴

1. **altruism** — unselfish concern for the welfare of others
2. **amber** — a pale yellow, red or brown fossil resin
3. **argyll diamond** — a yellowish diamond from the Argyll mines of Western Australia
4. **aspirational** — strong desire, longing or aim; taking an audible puff of breath before speaking, as in the *h* –sound
5. **attribute** — quality
6. **augment** — increase
7. **azure** — purplish shade of blue
8. **benign** — kindly
9. **booby-trap** — hidden bomb placed so it will be set off by an unsuspecting, innocent person
10. **bounty** — generous gift
11. **carnelian** — reddish semi–precious gemstone
12. **cerulean** — sky blue
13. **chrysoprase** — greenish semi–precious gemstone
14. **citrine** — lemonish or greenish semi–precious gemstone
15. **coincidence** — unusual occurrence of two events at the same time
16. **credentials** — evidence of authority

17.	**daffodil**	a trumpet-headed flower, usually bright yellow
18.	**disdain**	look on with contempt
19.	**emerald**	deep green gemstone
20.	**expel**	drive out by force
21.	**garnet**	deep red semi-precious gemstone
22.	**gibberish**	meaningless talk or writing
23.	**imitation**	copy or counterfeit
24.	**indulgence**	tolerance to a mood or whim
25.	**inferior**	lower in rank, station, position or quality
26.	**jade**	green semi-precious gemstone
27.	**jet**	semi-precious gemstone of black marble or polished coal
28.	**lavender**	pale bluish purple
29.	**lilac**	pale pinkish purple
30.	**lime**	lemonish green
31.	**mauve**	bluish purple
32.	**octave**	a tone on the eighth degree from another tone
33.	**olive**	brownish green
34.	**paean**	song of praise, joy or victory
35.	**peridot**	translucent green semi-precious gemstone
36.	**persimmon**	fruit of an orange-red colour

37. **plum**	fruit of a deep purplish colour
38. **predictive**	having an ability to foretell the future
39. **rubies**	translucent red gemstones
40. **rueful**	causing sorrow or pity
41. **sage**	wise person
42. **shuttle**	device used for weaving
43. **snortle**	laughter while snorting
44. **tangerine**	fruit of a bright orange colour
45. **tiger-eye**	banded semi-precious gemstone
46. **topaz**	translucent semi-precious gemstone
47. **trepidation**	trembling fear or alarm
48. **tribulation**	severe suffering
49. **violet**	purple of a reddish-blue shade
50. **violane**	rare violet or blue semi-precious gem

On the next page are diagrams showing different cuts for gemstones. Colour in the following gems with the correct colour (you may like to check on the internet beforehand—or consult *Daystar* to match the colour to the grace cloak) and label each one:

1. ruby
2. emerald
3. violane
4. argyll diamond
5. peridot
6. jet
7. garnet
8. topaz
9. citrine
10. carnelian
11. amber
12. jade
13. chyrsoprase
14. amethyst
15. rose quartz

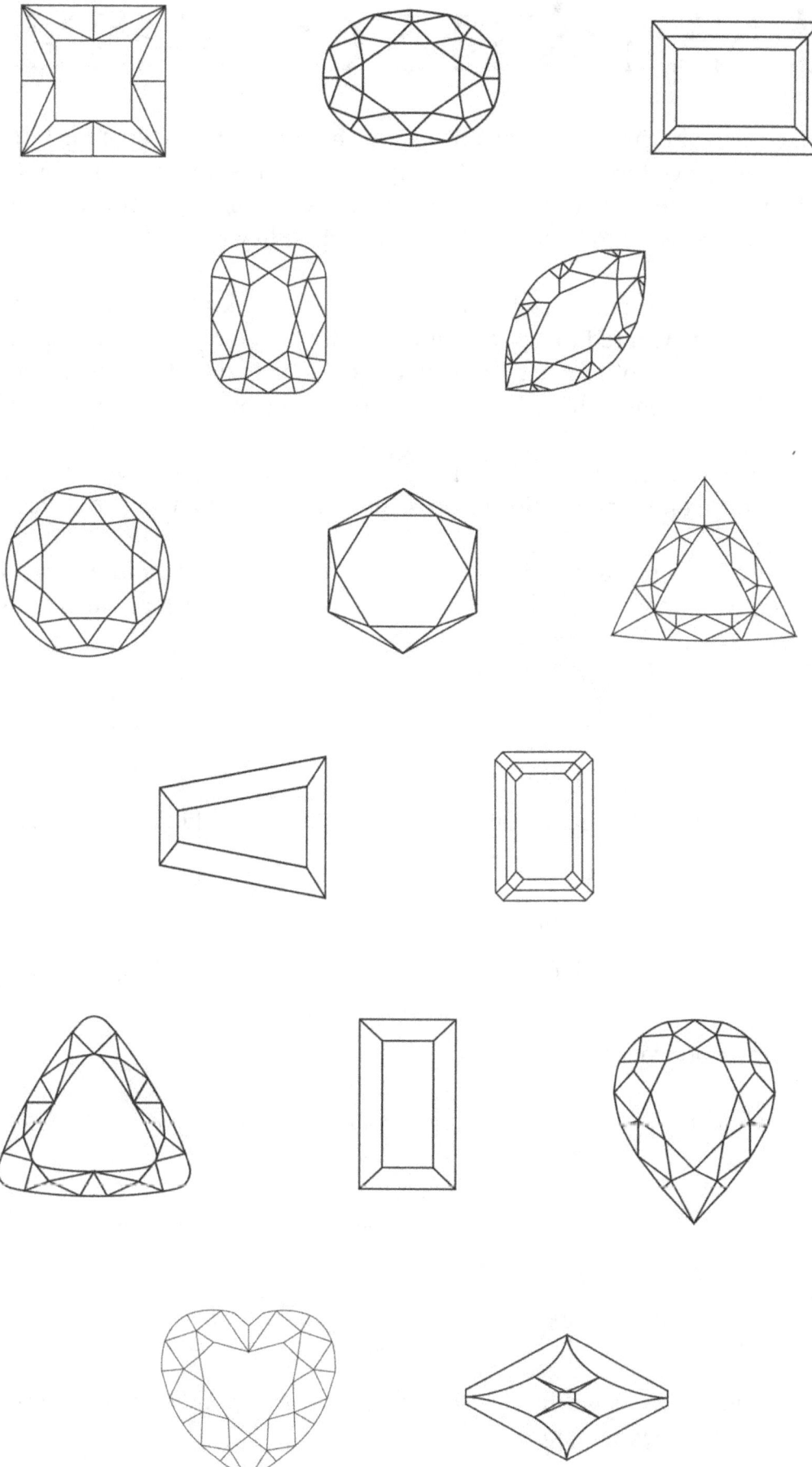

Inventing Words

'Snortle' is an invented word. It cannot be found in any standard dictionary such as the Oxford English dictionary. A good invented word is obvious in its meaning. Many writers have invented words over the centuries when there wasn't one ready to hand that fitted just what they wanted to say.

- Matthew the tax-collector, the writer of a book of the Bible named after him, wanted to describe how deeply affected Jesus was at seeing the distress of some sick people. So he invented the Greek word *splagchnizomai* which means 'gut–wrenching love'.

- William Shakespeare, one of the most famous English writers of all time, invented about 1700 words. Some of them might surprise you!

Here are 7 words we often use he made up:

Find another 7 words Shakespeare invented.

(1) lonely
(2) skim milk
(3) undress
(4) bloodstained
(5) champion
(6) blanket
(7) elbow

(8) ....
(9) ....
(10) ....
(11) ....
(12) ....
(13) ....
(14) ....

Now make up some words of your own:

A new colour: ....

A new item of clothing: ....

A new facial expression: ....

Ask some friends what they think your word means. It's a *good* invention, if their guess is a close one to what you intended.

Jewels of Poetry

Diamante design:

>**noun**
>adjective, adjective
>*verb, verb, verb*
>noun, noun, noun noun
>*verb, verb, verb*
>adjective, adjective
>**noun**

Example of a *Synonym Diamante*:

>Finches
>tiny, brown
>flying, circling, swirling
>wings, beaks, feathers, claws
>twirling, hopping, tweeting
>twitterish, secretive
>friends

Antonym Diamante example:
Dwarves and giants are opposites, or *antonyms*

>Dwarf
>short, sturdy
>battling, watching, seeking
>armour, disguise, guardian, warfare
>growling, planning, fighting
>powerful, tall
>Giant

Make up your own diamante poems. Choose from the following:

- **Synonym**: fox, marsh, castle, bridge, glacier, owl, sword, Flair

Antonym: peace and war; fire and water; king and servant

Vocabulary in Chapter F⁴

1. **amble** — go at a slow, easy pace
2. **defy** — challenge someone's power
3. **douse** — plunge into water or pour water on
4. **expendable** — able to be sacrificed to accomplish an objective
5. **hoarfrost** — needle-like ice crystals
6. **ignite** — set fire to
7. **incongruous** — out of place or keeping
8. **lullaby** — cradle song
9. **malevolence** — malice or hatred
10. **mephitic** — dark and poisonous
11. **mockery** — ridicule or contempt
12. **mutual** — common or shared
13. **panoply** — complete armour with accoutrements
14. **pathetic** — pitiful
15. **substitute** — replacement
16. **suffuse** — spread with colour or liquid
17. **talon** — claw
18. **temperamental** — forceful combination of mental and emotional traits exhibited by an individual

Draw the grace cloaks the dark Sleeper uses to transform itself.

WonderWord 13

Chapter F⁴ ~ Level: *medium*

Directions for words could be any of ⇒ ⇐ ⇑ ⇓ ↗ ↘ ↗ ↙

Y	S	W	O	R	D	M	G	P
E	H	H	U	T	G	A	R	R
L	I	E	O	L	N	I	A	O
L	E	L	R	E	O	L	C	G
O	L	M	A	B	S	C	E	I
W	D	E	N	P	E	O	U	D
L	E	T	G	E	H	A	L	N
G	R	E	E	N	T	T	B	I

(1) Find the words that fit in the missing spaces and describe the Seven Powers:

- Speaking ....
- Messenger ....
- .... of Veracity
- .... of Justice
- .... of Providence
- Daystar ....
- .... cloaks
- What holds the powers together (2 words)

(2) Find six of the seven colours of the grace cloaks.

(3) The leftover letters form the name of the seventh colour of the grace cloaks. What is the colour? ....

GINEVRA FAWN MASK ~

- Photocopy, increasing in size if necessary
- Paste on to stiff card
- Paint white and sprinkle with silver glitter
- Glue on whiskers
- Cut out the black eyes
- Punch out circles and loop rubber bands through them to hold on the ears

ORDER THE EVENTS 6

Order the events which occur while Ansey is guarding the gate of Ysgarde

1	Xerxes Xenophon explains his philosophy of business to Ansey.
2	Lally and Van ask to be allowed into the castle.
3	Hector and Emyr take a walk around the castle.
4	The Ancient of Days places a kiss on Ansey's shield.
5	Boody is wounded when she is mistaken for a bird of darkness.
6	A cowardly knight asks to take Ansey's place.
7	The Ancient of Days arrives and talks to Ansey.
8	Xerxes Xenophon arrives with Zippy.
9	Boody flies off to check out the castle.
10	Quystein hits Ansey for not opening the gate.
11	Xerxes Xenophon is revealed as a disguise of Uller Princekiller.
12	The raven Huginn points out that Ansey is guarding a gate.
13	Boody tries to warn the knights and dwarves about an ambush.
14	Lal and Van complain to Quystein about Ansey's stupidity.
15	The Days arrive back and explain how they smoked up the battle.
16	Munin wonders how he could understand the Ancient of Days.
17	Uller, ice-bound, watches the return of the Knights of Renown.
18	Ansey asks the gate to close.
19	Uller starts to turn into a snowman.
20	Ansey swaps the Speaking Sword for some slave children.

ORDER THE EVENTS 7

Order the events which occur when Fern tries to distract the Dark Sleeper

1	Fern throws the orange grace cloak over her shoulders.
2	The Dark Flyer transforms into a sea serpent—the Dark Dragon.
3	Fern gives the purple cloak to the Dark Dragon.
4	Fern drops the blue grace cloak to divert the Walker from a city.
5	The Dark Walker becomes the Dark Flyer.
6	Fern spins like a tornado around the Dark Walker.
7	Fern dives into the sea and discovers she can breathe underwater.
8	Fern hopes the Dark Dragon won't touch the yellow cloak.
9	Fern tries to hide the purple grace cloak.
10	Fern influences the Dragon to think the purple cloak is of kingship.
11	Fern throws her own indigo cloak at the Dragon's feet.
12	Fern realises the Dark Dragon is not following her.
13	Fern throws out the red grace cloak to gain a few seconds.
14	Fern puts the purple cloak on Emyr's shoulders for a moment.
15	Fern snatches a firestick from the ravens.
16	Fern decides not to drop the yellow grace cloak.
17	The Dark Dragon falls over, asleep.

Music of the Grace Cloaks

Consult the **musical score sheet**, where appropriate:

(1) What is another name for a minim?

(2) What is another name for a whole note?

(3) What is another name for a quarter note?

(4) What is another name for a quaver?

(5) What is another name for a semibreve?

(6) What is another name for a semi-quaver?

(7) What is another name for a whole rest?

(8) What is another name for a demi-semi-quaver?

(9) What is another name for a half note?

(10) What is another name for a sixteenth note?

(11) What is another name for a thirty-secondth note?

(12) What is another name for an eighth note?

(13) What is another name for a crotchet?

(14) What is another name for a semibreve rest?

(15) Find out what a treble clef is and draw one here.

(16) Draw a minim.

(17) Draw a crotchet.

(18) Draw a semibreve.

(19) Draw a semibreve rest.

(20) Draw a quaver.

(21) Draw a semi-quaver.

(22) Draw a demi-semi-quaver.

(23) Draw a whole note.

(24) Draw a half note.

(25) Draw a quarter note.

(26) Is a quarter note the same as a quaver?

(27) Find out what an octave is and write an explanation here:

Use coloured pens or pencils on the musical score sheet:

(28) Mark in the musical note hummed by the red grace cloak as a red crotchet.

(29) Mark in the musical note hummed by the yellow grace cloak as a yellow quaver.

(30) Mark in the musical note hummed by the indigo grace cloak as a midnight blue minim.

(31) Mark in the musical note hummed by the orange grace cloak as an orange semi-quaver.

(32) Mark in the musical note hummed by the purple grace cloak as a purple semibreve rest.

(33) Mark in the musical note hummed by the green grace cloak as a green semi-breve.

(34) Mark in the musical note hummed by the blue grace cloak as a blue semi-quaver.

(35) Mark in the musical note hummed by Ansey's grace cloak as a quaver. Choose the appropriate colour to match the cloak.

(36) Mark in the musical note hummed by Fern's grace cloak as a quaver. Choose the appropriate colour to match the cloak.

(37) Mark in the musical note hummed by Hector's grace cloak as a quaver. Choose the appropriate colour to match the cloak.

(38) Mark in the musical note hummed by Boody's grace cloak as a quaver. Choose the appropriate colour to match the cloak.

(39) Mark in the musical note hummed by Emyr's grace cloak as a quaver. Choose the appropriate colour to match the cloak.

(40) Mark in the musical note hummed by Birds and Fishes grace cloak as a quaver. Choose the appropriate colour to match the cloak.

(41) Mark in the musical note hummed by Sea and Sky grace cloak as a quaver. Choose the appropriate colour to match the cloak.

Make a Grace Cloak

Requirements:

- string
- scissors
- measuring tape
- ribbon
- fabric
- hemming tape
- fabric paints
- decorations
- chalk

- o **First**, decide what length of cloak you want:
    - a short cape that goes to your waist
    - a mantle that goes to your hips
    - a cloak to knees or ankles

- o **Second**, with a tape measure and a partner's help, find the distance from the top of your head to the bottom of the desired length of your cloak.

- o **Third**, go out and buy double that measurement of fabric in the solid colour you want. Buy four times the measurement in instant hemming tape.

- o **Fourth**, you need a pin, some chalk and a piece of string half the measurement of the fabric. (If you bought extra fabric, don't take the extra into account.)

- o **Fifth**, fold the fabric in half and pin the string to one folded corner. Pull it tight. It's to be used as a guide to make a quarter circle. Simply rotate it across the fabric and you will be able to draw a chalk circle. Cut along the chalked line. *Don't unfold the fabric yet!*

- o **Sixth**, measure the distance from the top of your head to your neck with string. Pin the string back in the same corner and make a chalk circle to cut out a space for your head. Once you've cut along the chalk line, you can unpin the string and unfold the fabric. You now have a half circle of fabric ready to hem.

- o **Seventh**, once you've used the instant hemming tape to neaten the top and bottom, sew on some ribbon across the top so you can tie the cloak together. Decorate it in colours that match the hue of the fabric. Using fabric paints, draw on musical notes.

Paint a Grace Cloak

Colour in your version of a grace cloak with its shimmering music.

APPLYING LOGIC

From the story, work out which colour cloak belongs to Ansey.

Apart from the information in the story, there is one other fact you need to know. Here it is:

*The **green** cloak belongs to **Ginevra** the white fawn.*

Now, using the table below, write in which character of the Seven Days has which gracecloak and work out which colour belongs to Ansey.

In no particular order, the Seven Days are: Hector, Fern, Emyr, Boody, Madmerry, Ansey and Ginevra.

Colour	Character
RED	
ORANGE	
YELLOW	
GREEN	
BLUE	
INDIGO	
VIOLET	

GEMSTONES

Amber, amethyst, aquamarine, argyll diamond, blue topaz, carnelian, citrine, emerald, garnet, jade, jet, lapis lazuli, lemon chrysoprase, peridot, ruby, sapphire, tiger-eye, topaz, violane

(1) Categorise the gemstones above according to their colour—use the hues of the stones on the grace cloaks in *Daystar* as a guide
(2) Research to find another gemstone, not listed above, which has a similar colour

Colour	Gemstones	Similar Colour
RED		
ORANGE		
YELLOW		
GREEN		
BLUE		
INDIGO		
VIOLET		

Do you have any of the gemstones above at home? Perhaps as a rock sample or in a birthstone ring or pendant?

What is the birthstone corresponding to the month you were born? ....

- Make a tally of the students in the class with the same birthstones.

Which birthday/birthstone is the most frequent? .... Least frequent? ....

- Graph the results in a pie graph using the gemstone colours.

Naming Days 3

A Surfeit of Princes

What does *surfeit* mean? ....

There are seven princes in the story but only four have been 'out-ed' so far. Which four are they?

A ....

E ....

G ....

T ....

Research:

What is the correct name for a group or collection of:

	Group name
Princes	
Finches	
Ravens	
Knights	
Giants	
Boys	
Girls	
Fish	

Threes

White Three at the White Tree: ....; ....; ....

Kinds of birds: o............s; ......n......h......s; ....v........s

Species: *humans; giants;* ....

Kings: R............n; M..............z; C..............e

CONFIDENTIAL!

Many of the characters in *Daystar* are keeping a secret. Match the person to the secret:

Candle	Is not a simple captain but the Commander of the Knights of Renown
Gratian	Is hiding one of the Seven Powers and wearing it under a decorated headpiece
Dallan	Knows where the secret entrance to the tunnel under the Wreathwatch Mountains is
Madmerry	Is hiding one of the Seven Powers and wearing it around his ankles
Hector	Is not a simple sheep-herder but the rightful king of Fyrzentsou
Uller	Has secretly practised swordplay when he was loaned a sword by an injured squire
Ansey	Has secretly collected seven grace cloaks and decides to risk all when he realises who The Days are
Maurtz	Knows the landscape is folding and wrinkling but is trying to hide it by using marble rollers to smooth out the lawns

Naming Days 4: Titles

1. Fill in the missing parts of Candle's title:

   Anointed High ...., Lord of The ...., Enthroned .... on the Rock of ...., Master of The .... Ways, Warden of the Scimitar ...., Well–builder of the ...., Son of .... and Child of .... Dream

2. Fill in Freutim's title:

   King of the .... Giants, Ruler of the .... Alliance

3. Fill in Gratian's title:

   Chief Prince of the .... Command of ....

4. Who has the title 'The White Three from the White Tree'?

   ....

5. What title does Uller give to Madmerry and Dallan?

   ....

6. Who becomes the 'Perfect Helper'?

   ....

7. Who is 'The King Who Guards the Gate'?

   ....

8. Who are the 'Days'?

   ....

9. A, B, C, D, E, F and G make up..

Collective Nouns

1. Match the following:

Single element	Group name
Day	Herd
Owl	Charm
Fox	Parliament
Deer	Skulk
Finch	Week
Raven	Platoon
Soldier	Storytelling

2. Cross out the wrong answer in each of the following:

   (a) An earth of foxes, a fury of foxes, a leash of foxes

   (b) A parcel of deer, a leash of deer, a darling of deer

   (c) A croak of ravens, an unkindness of ravens, a conspiracy of ravens

   (d) A team of horses, a harras of horses, a saddle of horses

   (e) A leap of leopards, a leep of leopards, a lope of leopards

   (f) A school of fish, a catch of fish, a frying of fish

   (g) A shield of knights, a banner of knights, a rout of knights

   (h) A spinney of trees, a grove of trees, a season of trees

   (i) A brigade of soldiers, a squad of soldiers, a squid of soldiers

   (j) A belt of asteroids, a band of asteroids, a twinkle of asteroids

3. Match the following:

Single element	Group name
Zebra	Badelynge
Chihuahua	Fluther
Hedgehog	Kendle
Cat	Prickle
Jellyfish	Yap
Duck	Zeal

The Armour of the Daystar

Match each piece of armour to the character who wears it. Be careful! There's a trick in the list.

Item of Armour	Character
helmet	Ansey
shoes	Boody
shield	Dallan
mailcoat	Fern
Belt	Ginevra
sword	Hector
lance	Madmerry

Vocabulary in Chapter G⁴

1. **dissipate** — scatter in various directions
2. **opposable** — able to be put in an opposite position
3. **pall** — covering of darkness
4. **portal** — door
5. **englobed** — placed within a globe
6. **limousine** — large, luxurious car

Your Opinion

Do you think the giants should be trusted? Give some reasons for your decision.

_____
_____
_____
_____

Do you think Uller Princekiller is truthful when he appears in the last chapter and explains the new danger? Justify your opinion.

_____
_____
_____

WHO SAID THAT?

Choose from the following list of speakers the character that made the statements quoted below.

Ancient of Days, Ansey, Boody, Candle, Dallan, Fern, Freutim, Ginevra, Gratian, Hector, Huginn, Madmerry, Munin, Nobble, Quystein, Stubble, Tobias, Uller, Wobble, Ysanne, a soldier of the King's Shield, the lift.

1. The land's cursed. It's folding in on itself.

2. A good king serves his people through his rule.

3. Those of us who get on with life find destiny seeking us out. We don't have to wait around for it, it's there waiting for us.

4. I always was a sucker for a prince with pretty manners.

5. Can you tell me if this is where I might find The King Who Guards The Gate?

6. Do you want healing for your heart or your soul?

7. Her weakness is the desire for beauty.

8. When the Days come, assuming their Power, then is the time unchancy late.

9. The Fifth Dwarf Legion at your service.

10. Seven Days do not make One Week, they simply are weak.

11. Uller Princekiller is my name, and royalty's passing is my game.

12. There is nothing in the entire universe, absolutely nothing, more terrifying than a nursery bogeyman that's even partly real.

13. Penthouse suite to your right. Have a nice day.

14. Wobble, Nobble, Monday, Tuesday, Wednesday, Thursday, Friday, Saturday and Sunday. Here to save the day. Which is obviously a brand new day, because the rest of the week is already accounted for.

15. You *can't* sell human beings. It's *not right*.

16. Grace cloaks don't actually exist. They're just legends from the time of tribulation after the Englobing.

17. Hey look, guys, I'm a *flying fox*!

18. Douse the lights, douse the lights.

19. Without the single heartbeat within this armour, without the single song in all its harmonic splendour shaping its form, this is a pile of useless junk.

20. What's the chance of getting a mobile phone of my own? I realised I don't need an opposable thumb to operate one.

Picky Pairs

Out of each pair of statements, pick the one that is **true**.

- Frost giants radiate cold; that's why it's chilly around them
- Frost giants pull heat from the air; that's why it's chilly around them

  - Dwarves and giants have been enemies for centuries
  - Dwarves and giants have been friends for centuries

- Ysgarde is anchored in the rock face at the top of a mountain pass
- Ysgarde rides on a pseudolithic cushion and only looks like it's built on rock

  - ☐ The Smoke Squadron used smoke to disturb the giants and ice up the field of battle
  - ☐ The Smoke Squadron used smoke to flush the trolls out of hiding and prevent an ambush

- There are no women fighters amongst the Knights of Renown
- There is at least one woman fighter in the Knights of Renown

  - Lord Quystein wanted to kill off the giants but Lord Ancelin wouldn't let him
  - Lord Quystein wanted to kill off the giants but Captain Gratian wouldn't let him

- The Acting Commander of the Knights of Renown is Quystein
- The Acting Commander of the Knights of Renown is Parment

  - ☐ Ansey faces three trials of his honour when he is guarding the gate
  - ☐ Ansey doesn't have to engage in any combat when he is guarding the gate

Some minor characters have their say on D✻A✻Y✻S✻T✻A✻R✻

'Rivetting. Enthralling. Superb. Beyond the best. Move over Tolkien. Simply the greatest epic fantasy ever: I laughed, I cried, I cheered out loud. I don't suppose anyone knows what I'm going to get paid for writing this endorsement?'
Xerxes Xenophon

'Unfortunately this fabulous flight of fantasy is flawed by a few far-fetched features: a "good" owl and some "heroic" ravens.'
An anonymous finch

'Full of Flair.'
Rigel & Mintaka, *horses*

'A travesty of a tale! Seven peace-loving wimps made to look like champions! Where were the wars, the great battles, the bloodchilling massacres? The fight against the manticores was over far too soon!'
Prince Tybold

'Soaring heroism, high adventure, knightly virtues, clever ruses, a race against time, a last desperate chance for peace—I loved it!'
Ysanne, *lady knight of Ysgarde*

'More Sevens than the seven times table. You get the impression there's a hidden mathematical side to this story.'
Tobias, *royal tutor*

'Adorable, agreeable, commendable, delectable, unforgettable!'
Nobble, *dwarf escort*

'Impeccable, invincible, incomparable, irresistible!'
Wobble, *dwarf escort*

'Noble!'
Stubble, *Commander of the Fifth Dwarf Legion*

Have *your* say:

....

....

....

Odd One Out

(1) Which of the following is not human?
    (a) Fern
    (b) Madmerry
    (c) Dallan
    (d) Hector

(2) Which of the following is not female?
    (a) Fern
    (b) Boody
    (c) Candle
    (d) Ginevra

(3) Which of the following is not male?
    (a) Candle
    (b) Gratian
    (c) Maurtz
    (d) Barbizca

(4) Which of the following is not a prince?
    (a) Tybold
    (b) Ansey
    (c) Emyr
    (d) Candle

(5) Which of the following is not one of Ansey's tutors?
    (a) Gratian
    (b) Tobias
    (c) Old Greywhiskers
    (d) Doctor Much

(6) Which of the following is not one of the White Three of the White Tree?
    (a) Hector
    (b) Boudicca's Chariot
    (c) Ginevra 'ayelet hashachar
    (d) Fern McDey

(7) Which of the following is not white?
    (a) Hector
    (b) Boudicca's Chariot
    (c) Ginevra 'ayelet hashachar
    (d) Madmerry

(8) Which of the following is not a dwarf?
- (a) Candle
- (b) Bramble
- (c) Rubble
- (d) Tobias

(9) Which of the following is not a kingdom?
- (a) Auberon
- (b) The White Tree
- (c) Fyrzentsou
- (d) Vircontium

(10) Which of the following is not royalty?
- (a) Ansey
- (b) Fern
- (c) Maurtz
- (d) Emyr

(11) Which of the following is not a feature of the landscape?
- (a) Harrowfell
- (b) Mistmurk
- (c) Wreathwatch Mountains
- (d) Ysgarde

(12) Which of the following do not attend Fern's school?
- (a) Elsa
- (b) Goliath
- (c) Cato
- (d) Uller

(13) Which of the following is not known to be available at the foodstalls in Auberon?
- (a) Venison pie
- (b) Blackbird pie
- (c) Fresh-baked bread
- (d) Hamburger

(14) Which of the following is not a bird?
- (a) Doody
- (b) Munin
- (c) Huginn
- (d) Uller

(15) Which of the following is not a horse?
- (a) Zippy
- (b) Rigel
- (c) Mintaka
- (d) Huginn

(16) Which of the following do not have Flair?
- (a) Fern
- (b) Madmerry
- (c) Ansey
- (d) Gratian

(17) Which of the following is not a giant?
- (a) Freutim
- (b) Uller
- (c) Munin
- (d) Huginn

(18) Which of the following is not a monster?
- (a) Manticores
- (b) Snow leopards
- (c) Snow demons
- (d) Dark Sleeper

(19) Which of the following is not a member of The Days?
- (a) Ansey
- (b) Boody
- (c) Candle
- (d) Dallan

(20) Which of the following is not the colour of a grace cloak?
- (a) Pink
- (b) Red
- (c) Green
- (d) Blue

(21) Which of the following is not a variety of giant?
- (a) Frost
- (b) Storm
- (c) Fire
- (d) Gas

(22) Which of the following is not a Knight of Renown?
- (a) Lord Quystein
- (b) Lady Ysanne
- (c) Ancelin of Tariquhaven
- (d) Freutim of the Jotun Alliance

(23) Which of the following was not given by The Song to Ansey?
- (a) A ring
- (b) A shield
- (c) A briefcase
- (d) Some fish

(24) Which of the following people did not visit Ansey while he was guarding the gate of Ysgarde?
- (a) Xerxes Xenophon
- (b) Lally and Van
- (c) Wreathwatch Woman
- (d) Rhodri Harke

(25) Which of the following was not given by Candle as a gift to The Days?
- (a) Sunglasses
- (b) Necklace
- (c) Sword
- (d) Cellphone

(26) Which of the following is not a sign that Fyrzentsou's true king has returned?
- (a) Rocks become perfumed
- (b) Mountainsides bloom with flowers
- (c) Firepetals fall from the sun
- (d) Jewels drop out of the sky

(27) Which of the following is not a member of the Smoke Squadron?
- (a) Ansey
- (b) Boody
- (c) Madmerry
- (d) Dallan

(28) Which of the following people is not wearing a disguise of some sort?
- (a) Xerxes Xenophon
- (b) Dallan
- (c) Madmerry
- (d) Ancelin Bedwyr Cai

(29) Which of the following is not a manifestation of the Dark Sleeper?
- (a) Flyer
- (b) Serpent
- (c) Dragon
- (d) Creeper

(30) Which of the following is not one of the Seven Powers?
- (a) Speaking Sword
- (b) Belt of Veracity
- (c) Messenger Shoes
- (d) Whispering Ring

Story Map

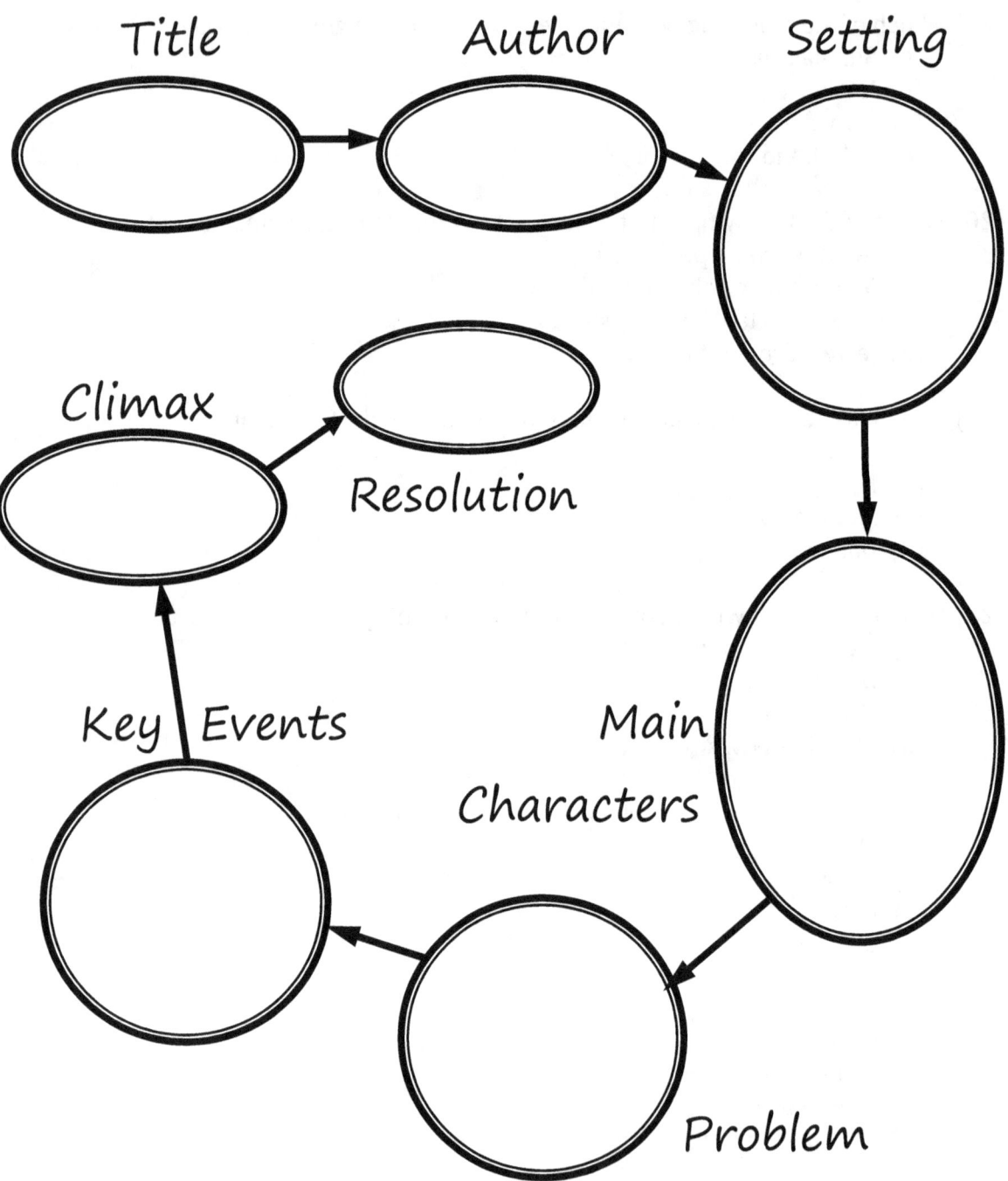

Teacher's Notes 3 from the **Author:**

Literary Influences on the story

JRR Tolkien

First up I have to mention Tolkien, the twentieth century's grand master of fantasy. I have a confession: it took me nearly three decades to finish *The Lord of The Rings*. Somewhere early in the story, I got completely confused between Sauron and Saruman and was of the belief that one was a fairly transparent disguise for the other. (I mean, Black Hand, White Hand; both commanded armies of orcs; both were evil watchers... you get the picture.) At some point, I realised they were entirely different and I'd got them inextricably entangled in my head. So I just gave up reading the book and didn't come back to it for almost thirty years. But I made a mental memo: don't give your main characters names that start with the same letter of the alphabet.

Hence the first germ of an idea to have an alphabetic sequence of names in *Daystar* came from this experience of getting muddled in what many consider to be the best book of the last century.

Raymond Alden

The genesis of *Daystar* began long ago when I read the short story, *The Knights of the Silver Shield* by Raymond Alden. From the moment I finished it, I knew that one day I would centre a story around the same theme. Then I lost my copy and for many years couldn't remember who the author was or what the proper title was. So I was absolutely delighted to rediscover the story in Rosie Boom's wonderful collection, *The Gift of Values Volume 1,* and to find it still had that same magic to thrill and exhalt my heart.

Ansey's crisis at the gate of Ysgarde—in fact, the entire *King Who Guards the Gate* sub-story—is entirely inspired by Alden's original. In addition, the properties of the silver shields of the Knights of Renown are lifted right out of it.

Is this kind of inspiration really just plagiarism? No. You may disagree but I'd like to suggest it's straight theft. TS Eliot said, 'Immature poets imitate, mature poets steal.' I hope I have, as Eliot suggested, not defaced Alden's work but paid homage to it by transforming it into something different but hopefully just as beautiful.

CS Lewis

For twenty years, I coordinated *Camp Narnia*, an annual holiday experience for upper primary students. Each day, we'd dramatise several (abridged) chapters from one of the *Chronicles of Narnia*. The campers would choose costumes from the costume box and act out the story as the narrator read it.

From those many dramatic presentations over the years, I learned the stories that go over best have
- a cast of thousands
- several main characters in a single group
- a sprinkling of talking animals

Lewis was at his best with a group of four main characters so I can't hold him responsible for giving me the idea to have seven of them. That inspiration is entirely due to the influence of...

GK Chesterton

The idea for The Days came from Chesterton's novel, *The Man Who Was Thursday*.

It is a surreal fantasy about a detective who infiltrates a group of anarchists (today they'd be terrorists) in order to discover their plans. He is given the codename *Thursday*. There are six other members of the plotting group, all with codenames from the days of the week. The twists and surprises are many as the detective seeks to foil the plans of the mysterious leader Sunday. The final revelation of who is on the side of good and who on the side of evil is, for me, stunning.

The idea for the grace cloaks comes from the scene towards the end of the story where the plotting group all find themselves guests of Sunday and provided with gifts of elaborately embroidered garments.

In his book, *Planet Narnia*, Michael Ward suggests that each of the books of the *Chronicles of Narnia* corresponds to the one of the planets of the medieval cosmos—planets that are somewhat different to our modern concept of the solar system. They are: Mercury, Venus, Mars, Jupiter, Saturn, Sun, Moon.

Now, as it happens, the days of the week are named after these seven planets:

- Sunday — after the sun
- Monday — after the moon
- Tuesday — after Tiw, the Anglo–Saxon equivalent of Mars
- Wednesday — after Woden, the Anglo–Saxon equivalent of Mercury
- Thursday — after Thor, the Anglo–Saxon equivalent of Jupiter
- Friday — after Freyja, the Anglo–Saxon equivalent of Venus
- Saturday — after Saturn

I need to be very clear here that this equivalence between Woden and Mercury and between Thor and Jupiter is an ancient one, going back to Julius Caesar's description of the Germanic tribal gods. Abandon the modern idea that Woden should parallel Jupiter because they were the heads of their respective pantheons! Instead favour, at least for the moment, the Roman view that Thor and Jupiter were the same because they were both quick-tempered deities who wielded lightning bolts and thunder hammers. Furthermore both Woden and Mercury were wily tricksters who acted as guides for the dead and were responsible for developing the art of writing.

I believe Michael Ward is correct in saying that the seven books of the *Chronicles of Narnia* have many planetary references in them. However, I also believe Lewis did not make any primary allusions to the planets in the series. They are secondary allusions. The chief and principal references are to the Days of the Week. These just happen to align with the seven medieval planets.

This means that, while Ward is correct in some of his identifications, he is wrong in others. Long before I was inspired to dip my imagination into *The Man Who Was Thursday* and pull out *Daystar*, I believe CS Lewis crafted the overarching theme of the *Chronicles of Narnia* on Chesterton's brilliant finale.

Much of Chesterton's work is difficult to read now because of its archaic language but *The Man Who Was Thursday* is worth persevering with because of its extraordinarily unexpected ending. It's an ending that many people do not like because a spy adventure suddenly turns into a philosophical fantasy. It's such an unexpected twist, even though there are hints along the way, that some people feel cheated. But I loved it. And it is to do with the nature of Days.

Lewis, I think, felt the pull of the questions Chesterton posed. And as it happens, with the exception of *The Horse and His Boy* (which was published much later than originally intended) and corresponds to Monday, I contend the *Chronicles of Narnia* follow the days of the week in order.

- *The Lion, the Witch and the Wardrobe* — Sunday
- *Prince Caspian* — Tuesday
- *The Voyage of the Dawn Treader* — Wednesday
- *The Silver Chair* — Thursday
- *The Horse and His Boy* — Monday
- *The Magician's Nephew* — Friday
- *The Last Battle* — Saturday

I should point out that, out of the Chronicles, the biggest influence on *Daystar* has been *The Silver Chair*, the book of Thursday. Although Thursday is named after Thor, 'thurs' itself is a Norse word for *giant* and Lewis, it seems, could never resist a good pun. Another Norse word is for *giant* is 'jotun' which passed into Middle English as 'ettin'. *The Silver Chair* is replete with giants, from Ettinsmoor to Harfang.

The courteous devious giants of Harfang had considerable impact on the character of Uller Princekiller.

Barry Hughart

There's a line, spoken by Hector in *Daystar*, that is a sentiment borrowed from one of Barry Hughart's books. I think, but I'm not entirely sure, it was *Bridge of Birds*. (You can tell from the age of these references how long ago *Daystar* was first conceived.) The sentiment is this: *there's nothing in the universe, absolutely nothing, more frightening than a nursery bogeyman that's even half real.*

In my childhood, I suffered from nightmares a lot. As an adult, I've discovered that the figures in those nightmares are nursery bogeymen from another time and place. There's something genuinely disturbing about being able to trace a hidden family heritage, more than seven generations distant, through the 'genius loci' of a nightmare. Which is why I put these words in Hector's mouth.

Michael Scott Rohan

I think it was in the front of a book by Michael Scott Rohan that I saw a map which had printed in one corner: 'Country of the Frost Giants'. I think the book was part of a trilogy or perhaps even a series. A pity there were no frost giants in the actual story (though there may have been in the wider series, had I gone on to pursue it) because this seemed an extremely evocative and intriguing name.

At first, I had no intention of featuring a frost giant in the story. The character was meant to be a nameless bit of exotic background colour at the fair where Ansey meets Fern and the other Days.

Some authors will tell you of their experiences with characters who become so real they seem to come alive and argue with the author; while others suggest this is a sign of bad planning in the characterisation department. I don't like to be so prescriptive about my characters. I like to leave room for them to surprise me. To start with, Uller was supposed to be an anonymous frost giant, a character who never even opened his mouth. Once I made the mistake of letting him talk to Ansey, he simply walked off with the story and took it in quite a different direction.

Once he was a major character, I had to give him a name and also to find out more about frost giants which, back in the days before Google, was no easy task. However, I never had the slightest inclination to go back to Michael Scott Rohan. Still, I have to credit him with seeding the phrase in my mind.

I find it hugely ironic that one of the most important characters in the book, Uller Princekiller, was inspired by a few words on a map. The vast majority of fantasy readers love maps. I don't like them. I so much loathe them in fact that the plot of *Daystar* (and also, by the way, of *Many-Coloured Realm*) was designed so that no map could be drawn which would accurately represent the world I was depicting.

I heard Russell Fitzpatrick speak on map-making in 2010 at the World Science Fiction Convention in Melbourne. His view of maps was such an eye-opener that I actually changed my mind about them. But the plot of *Daystar* had been set for nearly two decades so, although it's possible to draw a map, it would only be accurate for a moment in time.

Madeleine L'Engle

It's a strange thing but I like Madeleine L'Engle's non-fiction much better than I like her fiction. Even within her fantasy writings, I much prefer *A Swiftly Tilting Planet* to her acclaimed classic *A Wrinkle in Time*. My favourite of all her works is *Walking on Water* in which she writes about writing and shuttles back and forward, like a weaver, on various topics. The one that has influenced me the most is her concept of Naming.

L'Engle articulated ideas that were dreaming inside me. Her discussion of Naming told me why I felt it necessary to find the right name for the character and spend time other writers felt was better used in actually writing.

I've come a long way from the time she awakened my nascent sense of the importance of names, even for characters in a fantasy adventure. I've looked at the patterns of naming in many books, my own included. I've researched what the act of naming meant long ago and looked into the notion of the 'power of names'—as well as the ancient concept that names reflect both identity and destiny and that what you are called signifies your calling.

It isn't very long before you realise that, in fantasy—as in no other genre—the ancient view that names as carriers of destiny is alive and well. The patterns of naming in modern fantasy are, if the writer has spent any time on them at all, as old as the oldest literature. The resonant sense that they are shines through: L'Engle herself, her name coming from the word for *angel*, has a recurring motif of the cherubim; Lewis, from the Welsh for *lion* which derives from the name of the Celtic god of light, redefines his symbolic lion in a finely-tuned way.

The topic of naming is so massive that even the surface cannot be scratched here. If you are interested in learning more, I draw your attention to my book, *God's Poetry: The Identity and Destiny Encoded in Your Name*, available from Even Before Publishing. One chapter of the book looks at the concept of naming in modern fantasy.

Dallan Forgaill

In the very first draft of the story, I used the name 'Dallan' because I discovered it in a book of names with no other information other than that it was a rare Irish name and it meant *blind*. As one of the characters was seriously visually impaired and he was hiding his true identity, it seemed like a good choice for him. It is a name, however, that has never 'felt' right.

As I've mentioned above, I put a lot of store by names and their fittingness within a story. I will spend months searching for the right name for a character, poring over lists of names and meanings, and never consider this exercise a waste of time. A lot of authors I know think it's time better spent writing, so I always considered this a curious quirk in my make-up. I knew Madeleine L'Engle considered Naming as enormously important but I doubted even she spent as long as I did searching for the perfect name. Only a few writers I've met felt the same way but I was very reassured when I was at a conference where Michael Morpurgo was the guest. 'It's sounds pathetic,' he said, 'but until I get the right name for my characters, I can hardly write a thing.'

The odd thing about Dallan is that the name never quite 'felt' right. It still doesn't, to a degree.

However, there is a sense in which it is perfect. And it certainly has had an impact on the direction of the last draft.

In 2010, I spent a month in the north of Ireland. One day I saw in a brochure a single line about a town I'd passed through: *Outside Limavady is the site of the Convocation of Drum Ceatt.*

Now I've always loved the story of Drum Ceatt and Columba's return to Ireland. It has a wonderful element from a story-telling point of view: a man of integrity who has made an unbreakable vow now he realises what an appalling bind he has put himself in.

It was the mid-sixth century. Columba had exiled himself from Ireland after causing a battle in which many of his friends were killed. (It was a result of the first case of copyright infringement, but that's another story.) On leaving for Scotland, where he eventually established a monastery on Iona, he swore never to set foot on Irish soil again or even to look on her fair shores. Indeed, it's possible to see Ireland on a clear day from almost every island off the west coast of Scotland south of Iona, but not from Iona itself.

A few years went by and back in Ireland, the bards got a bit uppity. These privileged poets were a class of scholars whose learning and skills were originally part of the old druid colleges. They were used to being rewarded handsomely for their songs, especially those with lyrics that happened to exalt kings and so ensure their names would live down the ages. Now one day, one of the bards at the royal court asked the High King, Aed, for the royal gold torc around his neck as a reward. It'd be like asking the queen for her crown today: it was presumption and arrogance of the highest order.

Aed was outraged. The court bards were incensed by his reaction. Aed refused to hand over the torc. The bards were furious. Aed threatened to exile them. In turn, the bards threatened to perform *roscad*: to satirise the king so that he would be a laughingstock throughout history.

This might not sound like much of a threat today but it was very serious back then when honour was so important and words were seen as alive: once spoken, their power was active and unable to be revoked. Not to be outdone, Aed threatened to exile every last bard in Ireland, saying they were simply druids pretending to be Christians.

Imagine it! Ireland, the land of poetry and song, was about to be deprived of its music. Someone got to Aed and persuaded him to let the case be decided at the Convocation of Drum Ceatt.

Drum Ceatt is, according to many descriptions of it, a daisy-covered hill just outside Limavady. Well, it might have been once. But, as I discovered when I spent most of a day driving around the countryside looking for it, it is manicured and green, with a crown of gorse, in the middle of a golf course.

It was Columba's return to Ireland and his persuasive argument for clemency for the bards at Drum Ceatt that turned the tide. And no, he didn't break his vow to do it. He'd sworn never to set foot on Irish soil again, so he tied clods of Scottish turf to his feet and walked on them the whole time. He'd sworn never to look on the fair shores of Ireland again, so he wore a blindfold.

No doubt Aed was impressed when he turned up to make a plea on behalf of the bards. Certainly he agreed not to exile them.

Now you may think I've got side-tracked here and have forgotten that this was supposed to be about Dallan Forgaill. Not at all. Dallan is the quiet, unassuming man-behind-the-scenes in all this.

He was a monk who lived on an island just off the coast of Donegal. However he was also the chief of all the bards of Ireland and thus, it seems very likely, a convert from druidism. It's difficult to explain how he could have held this position unless he had studied with the druids. Although he seems to have had nothing to do with the altercation between Aed and his court bards, he is probably the one who sent a message to Columba and asked him to come and speak at Drum Ceatt. It was a cunning move. Columba had been a prince of the O'Neill and would certainly be seen as less biassed than Dallan himself with his background.

Columba's eloquence thus staved off the prospect of all the songs of Ireland being stilled. He consequently ensured the preservation of a song by Dallan

Forgaill himself: the famous lorica translated in the nineteenth century as *Be Thou My Vision.*

Be Thou My Vision is an interesting hymn in that it has two different versions of the third verse. It's only when you notice this and look at the original translation that you become aware of the massive shift in thinking between the nineteenth and the twenty-first century. Dallan Forgaill's original sixth-century Gaelic versification does not use words about armour in their sense of the outfitting of a warrior. Rather, he used words about armour in their sense of an essential element of covenant exchange: to do with the concept of Oneness and blood brotherhood.

The new third verse removes the words 'dignity' and 'delight' and is about fighting. The old third verse in using 'dignity' and 'delight' points directly to the ancient ideas of covenantal Oneness. This is re-iterated in the repeated words: 'heart of my own heart' and 'I with Thee one'.

I've always been concerned about the promotion of violence in fantasy, both overtly and tacitly. One of the themes of *Daystar* is peace: not as the aftermath of war but as a state of mind that seeks to prevent wars and to reconcile. Apart from the fight with the manticores, there aren't any big battles in *Daystar*. This is deliberate.

This is why, when I discovered that I'd set myself up perfectly (but unknowingly) through two dozen drafts by having a character named Dallan, that in the final draft *Be Thou My Vision* became an integral part of the story.

John de Massey

It's a real pity that I don't know for sure the name of the author to whom I am most indebted. I'm going to call him John de Massey because constantly referring to him as 'the anonymous author of the fourteenth century poem, *Sir Gawain and the Green Knight*' will get to be very wearing very quickly. So, bear in mind, his name may not be John de Massey, even though I think it probably is.

John is the author of seven works. Now I know that many experts in medieval literature will dispute that statement. However I believe his stories are: *Sir Gawain and the Green Knight, Pearl, Patience, Purity* (also called *Cleanness*), *St Erkenwald, Summer Sunday* (also called *Fortune*) and *Death and Liffe*. Apart from the fact that all these narrative poems are actually in the same dialect, they have a mathematical design underneath them that is so similar that I consider it a 'signature'. It's very distinctive and so unusual that I believe it's safe to say John is the author of all the works mentioned above.

Ed Condren, professor at UCLA, in *The Numerical Universe of the Gawain-Pearl Poet: Beyond Phi* (University Press of Florida, 2002) makes a superb case for the first four poems all being John's but I believe the last three can be added as well.

Almost all of what I know about word-number fusions and numerical literary design (so called by Maarten Menken and Joost Smit Sibinga, but also called 'Biblical style' (Howlett), 'structural arithmetic metaphor' (Bulatkin), 'architectonics' (Crawford), 'arithmology' or 'arithmetic theology' (Røstvig) and mathematical metaphor by myself) comes from examining John's work. He wasn't just a poet, he was a theologian and an apologist and a mathematician.

Creativity in our time has become associated with freedom of expression and style. This was not always the case. In classical Greece, ideals of beauty constrained all artistic forms including poetry and story-telling. These ideals were mathematical in nature and were based on the 'perfect' proportions of the human body. One writer broke off his story with an apology for failing to end it but saying he had strayed outside the due limits. The same writer in another place apologised for his transgression but said he had to finish the story anyway.

The Greek New Testament uses this idea of numerical literary style (words within a careful mathematical design) but with a unique spin. It was a natural progression from the rich mathematical structure of the Hebrew scriptures—the word for 'scribes' in Hebrew and Aramaic did not mean 'counters' without reason. For thousands of years, until the sixteenth century, words and numbers were not seen as separate but as deeply and profoundly connected.

John's poems may well be the pinnacle of this style, the last spectacular blooming before it abruptly disappeared a century later. Two of his narratives—*Sir Gawain and the Green Knight* and *Pearl*—are acknowledged as being amongst the finest English literature of all time.

Both CS Lewis and Tolkien immensely admired his work. Tolkien translated both *Pearl* and *Sir Gawain and the Green Knight* into modern English. (While this is a very fine translation, my current favourite version of the latter is Burton Raffel's which, I think, preserves the rollicking sense of fun in the original.) Lewis referred to Gawain when talking about Jack the giant killer. He also alluded to the story in *The Silver Chair* where Gawain's hostess, the *Lady of the Green Girdle*, makes a sinuous morph into *The Lady of the Green Kirtle*.

In his effect on the writings of Tolkien and Lewis (whose books were consistently voted most popular in polls taken at the end of the twentieth century), John may possibly be the most influential writer of the last millennium.

So it's fortunate the one and only copy of his work survived the centuries to come to light in the mid-nineteenth century and then become available for people like Tolkien and Lewis to fall in love with it. Michael Morpurgo, former children's laureate, credits the poem *Sir Gawain and the Green Knight* with re-awakening his love of story.

Now apart from stealing John's mathematical design principles for *Daystar* which is 77777 words long, I've also stolen an idea I discovered in his arithmetic metaphors. Perhaps the most famous section of *Sir Gawain and the Green Knight* is the long description of Gawain's shield which is part of an even longer Arming Sequence in which Gawain is girded in a knight's armour. Within the mathematical architecture of the manuscript, there are several 'golden sections', one of which occurs here and another of which occurs in the poem *Patience* where there is an allusion to the Kiss of Heaven and Earth.

Initially this seemed extremely odd. Armour linked to a kiss?

However, there was one obvious starting point: the description of the Armour of God in Ephesians 6. Spend thirty seconds there and you realise that Truth, Peace, Righteousness and Mercy—the elements of the medieval Kiss of Heaven and Earth—are indeed present. Spend a little longer in looking into the mathematical value of the sequence and you'll find it is 77792. I expected it to be 77777 if it was indeed the Kiss of Heaven and Earth and took a moment to account for the difference: 77792 is divisible by 17 and 22, which 77777 is not. The significance and predominance of 17 in early Christian writing is too complex a subject to tackle here. The significance and predominance of 22 to Hebrew thinking is also too complex a subject to tackle here. (However, if you'd really like to know more about them, see my book *Gawain and the Four Daughters of God: the testimony of mathematics in Cotton Nero A.x.*)

It was clear John had got his mathematics (with its ubiquitous 17 and its frequent 22) and his idea to connect the Armour and the Kiss from Paul of Tarsus.

I guess most people would have left it at that. But I went: 'What!? What on earth were you thinking, Paul? A kiss and armour? Like they're somehow equivalent? How weird is that!'

In fact, Paul, a self-confessed Hebrew of the Hebrews, was having a very Jewish thought. In Aramaic, the word for *to kiss* is conceptually the same word as *to put on armour*. To put on the armour of God is to lift your face for the kiss of God.

The resolution of the crisis in *Daystar* revolves around this hidden idea just as John's four most well-known poems—*Pearl*, *Purity*, *Patience* and *Sir Gawain and the Green Knight*—have this theme hidden in their mathematical superstructure.

As for peace, mercy, truth and righteousness, they are of course present in *Daystar* too.

Its setting in a world with medieval European overtones is not simply so that armour would naturally appear in the story but also because this was the last time when the word and number fusion I have used in the story was widely used. It was the last time when knowledge was integrated across a curriculum. We live in a world of data and information. Knowledge comes with the ability to put the information together in meaningful ways. Wisdom comes when we are able to put knowledge together in meaningful ways.

We have lost the ability to do that with our fragmentation into every more specialised subject areas.

77777 is divisible by 7, 41, 271 and 11111. It was a pity it wasn't divisible by 101 (a number favoured by John de Massey for its symbolism as a metaphor for the Music of the Spheres) but it was only 7 away. John would have understood why I went for 77777 instead of 77770. He often had to make such choices himself.

Now John would have thought my numerical literary work to be very basic and utterly transparent. To a medieval mind, I really haven't got out of kindergarten with 77777, I've lacked subtlety and I've presented my metaphors with all the finesse of a sledgehammer. However, for a postmodern mind, I'm talking such a completely different language that my metaphors need to be explained. And here they are:

- 7 for the days of the week, the colours of the rainbow, the notes of the musical scale and the number of pieces in the divine armour.
- 11111 for 'covenant'—the essential nature of which is *not* contract, but oneness.
- 101 (not quite but almost) because, without the Music of the Spheres to complete the panoply in the story, it just didn't seem quite right.

Story Summary:

Ansey's great desire is to be a knight and to serve others. His father, the king of Auberon, is dead set against this ambition. Auberon is under threat: the landscape is folding due to earthshakes and sub-surface tremors.

During sports day at school, Fern is catapulted into Auberon and, to her surprise, finds she understands the language of Boody the white owl, Ginevra the white fawn and Hector the white fox. The animals decide she is the 'Perfect Helper', sent to save Auberon and the other kingdoms. They set off to find the king but instead encounter Ansey and the masked herbalist Madmerry and her autistic friend, Dallan.

Ansey is captured by Uller Princekiller, a frost giant. In the ensuing chaos after his abduction, Fern and her new friends try to escape Auberon. They are attacked by Ansey's companion, the dwarf Candle, and by manticores—blood-coloured lions with human faces and scorpion tails. They are aided by a strange visitor who calls himself 'The Song' and assaulted by the vicious Snow Queen who has woven Dallan's fate to her own.

Unexpectedly saved by Uller, they discover that they may be the embodiment of an ancient prophecy about the Seven Days. As it gradually emerges that they are the Children of Light, they face increasing opposition from their own side. Everyone has been expecting mighty warriors, masterful sages or powerful magicians will be the ones to protect them against the evil Children of Night. Not a bunch of innocent, useless kids.

But the Days surprise everyone, themselves included. Only they have the seven powers it takes to defeat the Darkness: faith, justice, truth, peace, redemption, word of honour—and, binding all together, The Song.

The Knights of the Silver Shield

From the collection, *Why the Chimes Rang*, Raymond Macdonald Alden 1908

THERE WAS ONCE A SPLENDID CASTLE in a forest, with great stone walls and a high gateway, and turrets that rose away above the tallest trees. The forest was dark and dangerous, and many cruel giants lived in it; but in the castle was a company of knights, who were kept there by the king of the country, to help travellers who might be in the forest, and to fight with the giants whenever they could.

Each of these knights wore a beautiful suit of armour and carried a long spear, while over his helmet there floated a great red plume that could be seen a long way off by any one in distress. But the most wonderful thing about the knights' armour was their shields. They were not like those of other knights, but had been made by a great magician who had lived in the castle many years before. They were made of silver, and sometimes shone in the sunlight with dazzling brightness; but at other times the surface of the shields would be clouded as though by a mist, and one could not see his face reflected there as he could when they shone brightly.

Now, when each young knight received his spurs and his armour, a new shield was also given him from among those that the magician had made; and when the shield was new its surface was always cloudy and dull. But as the knight began to do service against the giants, or went on expeditions to help poor travellers in the forest, his shield grew brighter and brighter, so that he could see his face clearly reflected in it. But if he proved to be a lazy or cowardly knight, and let the giants get the better of him, or did not care what became of the travellers, then the shield grew more and more cloudy, until the knight became ashamed to carry it.

But this was not all. When any one of the knights fought a particularly hard battle, and won the victory, or when he went on some hard errand for the lord of the castle, and was successful, not only did his silver shield grow brighter, but when one looked into the centre of it he could see something like a golden star shining in its very heart. This was the greatest honour that a knight could achieve, and the other knights always spoke of such a one as having 'won his star.' It was usually not till he was pretty old and tried as a soldier that he could win it. At the time when this story begins, the lord of the castle himself was the only one of the knights whose shield bore the golden star.

There came a time when the worst of the giants in the forest gathered themselves together to have a battle against the knights. They made a camp in a dark hollow not far from the castle, and gathered all their best warriors together, and all the knights made ready to fight them. The windows of the castle were closed and barred; the air was full of the noise of armour being made ready for use; and the knights were so excited that they could scarcely rest or eat.

Now there was a young knight in the castle, named Sir Roland, who was among those most eager for the battle. He was a splendid warrior, with eyes that shone like stars whenever there was anything to do in the way of knightly deeds. And although he was still quite young, his shield had begun to shine enough to show plainly that he had done bravely in some of his errands through the forest. This battle, he thought, would be the great opportunity of his life. And on the morning of the day when they were to go forth to it, and all the knights assembled in the great hall of the castle to receive the commands of their leaders, Sir Roland hoped that he would be put in the most dangerous place of all, so that he could show what knightly stuff he was made of.

But when the lord of the castle came to him, as he went about in full armour giving his commands, he said: 'One brave knight must stay behind and guard the gateway of the castle, and it is you, Sir Roland, being one of the youngest, whom I have chosen for this.'

At these words Sir Roland was so disappointed that he bit his lip, and closed his helmet over his face so that the other knights might not see it. For a moment he felt as if he must reply angrily to the commander, and tell him that it was not right to leave so sturdy a knight behind, when he was eager to fight. But he struggled against this feeling, and went quietly to look after his duties at the gate. The gateway was high and narrow, and was reached from outside by a high, narrow bridge that crossed the moat, which surrounded the castle on every side. When an enemy approached, the knight on guard rang a great bell just inside the gate, and the bridge was drawn up against the castle wall, so that no one could come across the moat. So the giants had long ago given up trying to attack the castle itself.

Today the battle was to be in the dark hollow in the forest, and it was not likely that there would be anything to do at the castle gate, except to watch it like a common doorkeeper. It was not strange that Sir Roland thought someone else might have done this.

Presently all the other knights marched out in their flashing armour, their red plumes waving over their heads, and their spears in their hands. The lord of the castle stopped only to tell Sir Roland to keep guard over the gate until they had all returned, and to let no one enter. Then they went into the shadows of the forest, and were soon lost to sight.

Sir Roland stood looking after them long after they had gone, thinking how happy he would be if he were on the way to battle like them. But after a little he put this out of his mind, and tried to think of pleasanter things. It was a long time before anything happened, or any word came from the battle.

At last Sir Roland saw one of the knights come limping down the path to the castle, and he went out on the bridge to meet him. Now this knight was not a brave one, and he had been frightened away as soon as he was wounded.

'I have been hurt,' he said, 'so that I cannot fight any more. But I could watch the gate for you, if you would like to go back in my place.'

At first Sir Roland's heart leaped with joy at this, but then he remembered what the commander had told him on going away, and he said:

'I should like to go, but a knight belongs where his commander has put him. My place is here at the gate, and I cannot open it even for you. Your place is at the battle.'

The knight was ashamed when he heard this, and he presently turned about and went into the forest again.

So Sir Roland kept guard silently for another hour. Then there came an old beggar woman down the path to the castle, and asked Sir Roland if she might come in and have some food. He told her that no one could enter the castle that day, but that he would send a servant out to her with food, and that she might sit and rest as long as she would.

'I have been past the hollow in the forest where the battle is going on,' said the old woman, while she was waiting for her food.

'And how do you think it is going?' asked Sir Roland.

'Badly for the knights, I am afraid,' said the old woman. 'The giants are fighting as they have never fought before. I should think you had better go and help your friends.'

'I should like to, indeed,' said Sir Roland. 'But I am set to guard the gateway of the castle, and cannot leave.'

An old beggar woman came down the path

'One fresh knight would make a great difference when they are all weary with fighting,' said the old woman. 'I should think that, while there are no enemies about, you would be much more useful there.'

'You may well think so,' said Sir Roland, 'and so may I; but it is neither you nor I that is commander here.'

'I suppose,' said the old woman then, 'that you are one of the kind of knights who like to keep out of fighting. You are lucky to have so good an excuse for staying at home.' And she laughed a thin and taunting laugh.

Then Sir Roland was very angry, and thought that if it were only a man instead of a woman, he would show him whether he liked fighting or no. But as it was a woman, he shut his lips and set his teeth hard together, and as the servant came just then with the food he had sent for, he gave it to the old woman quickly, and shut the gate that she might not talk to him anymore.

It was not very long before he heard someone calling outside. Sir Roland opened the gate, and saw standing at the other end of the drawbridge a little old man in a long black cloak. 'Why are you knocking here?' he said. 'The castle is closed today.'

'Are you Sir Roland?' said the little old man.

'Yes,' said Sir Roland.

'Then you ought not to be staying here when your commander and his knights are having so hard a struggle with the giants, and when you have the chance to make of yourself the greatest knight in this kingdom. Listen to me! I have brought you a magic sword.'

As he said this, the old man drew from under his coat a wonderful sword that flashed in the sunlight as if it were covered with diamonds. 'This is the sword of all swords,' he said, 'and it is for you, if you will leave your idling here by the castle gate, and carry it to the battle. Nothing can stand before it. When you lift it the giants will fall back, your master will be saved, and you will be crowned the victorious knight—the one who will soon take his commander's place as lord of the castle.'

Now Sir Roland believed that it was a magician who was speaking to him, for it certainly appeared to be a magic sword. It seemed so wonderful that the sword should be brought to him, that he reached out his hand as though he would take it, and the little old man came forward, as though he would cross the drawbridge into the castle. But as he did so, it came to Sir Roland's mind again that that bridge and the gateway had been entrusted to him, and he called out 'No!' to the old man, so that he stopped where he was standing. But he waved the shining sword in the air again, and said: 'It is for you! Take it, and win the victory!'

Sir Roland was really afraid that if he looked any longer at the sword, or listened to any more words of the old man, he would not be able to hold himself within the castle. For this reason he struck the great bell at the gateway, which was the signal for the servants inside to pull in the chains of the drawbridge, and instantly they began to pull, and the drawbridge came up, so that the old man could not cross it to enter the castle, nor Sir Roland to go out.

Then, as he looked across the moat, Sir Roland saw a wonderful thing. The little old man threw off his black cloak, and as he did so he began to grow bigger and bigger, until in a minute more he was a giant as tall as any in the forest. At first Sir Roland could scarcely believe his eyes. Then he realized that this must be one of their giant enemies, who had changed himself to a little old man through some magic power, that he might make his way into the castle while all the knights were away. Sir Roland shuddered to think what might have happened if he had taken the sword and left the gate unguarded. The giant shook his fist across the moat that lay between them, and then, knowing that he could do nothing more, he went angrily back into the forest.

Sir Roland now resolved not to open the gate again, and to pay no attention to any other visitor. But it was not long before he heard a sound that made him spring forward in joy. It was the bugle of the lord of the castle, and there came sounding after it the bugles of many of the knights that were with him, pealing so joyfully that Sir Roland was sure they were safe and happy. As they came nearer, he could hear their shouts of victory. So he gave the signal to let down the drawbridge again, and went out to meet them. They were dusty and bloodstained and weary, but they had won the battle with the giants; and it had been such a great victory that there had never been a happier home–coming.

Sir Roland greeted them all as they passed in over the bridge, and then, when he had closed the gate and fastened it, he followed them into the great hall of the castle. The lord of the castle took his place on the highest seat, with the other knights about him, and Sir Roland came forward with the key of the gate, to give his account of what he had done in the place to which the commander had appointed him. The lord of the castle bowed to him as a sign for him to begin, but just as he opened his mouth to speak, one of the knights cried out:

'The shield! the shield! Sir Roland's shield!'

Every one turned and looked at the shield which Sir Roland carried on his left arm. He himself could see only the top of it, and did not know what they could mean. But what they saw was the golden star of knighthood, shining brightly from the centre of Sir Roland's shield. There had never been such amazement in the castle before.

Sir Roland knelt before the lord of the castle to receive his commands. He still did not know why everyone was looking at him so excitedly, and wondered if he had in some way done wrong.

'Speak, Sir Knight,' said the commander, as soon as he could find his voice after his surprise, 'and tell us all that has happened today at the castle. Have you been attacked? Have any giants come hither? Did you fight them alone?'

'No, my Lord,' said Sir Roland. 'Only one giant has been here, and he went away silently when he found he could not enter.'

Then he told all that had happened through the day.

When he had finished, the knights all looked at one another, but no one spoke a word. Then they looked again at Sir Roland's shield, to make sure that their eyes had not deceived them, and there the golden star was still shining.

After a little silence the lord of the castle spoke.

'Men make mistakes,' he said, 'but our silver shields are never mistaken. Sir Roland has fought and won the hardest battle of all to-day.'

Then the others all rose and saluted Sir Roland, who was the youngest knight that ever carried the golden star.

COMPREHENSION

1) Describe the armour of the Knights of the Silver Shield:

    (i) They carried a long ……………….

    (ii) They wore a helmet with ……………………………

    (iii) They had a special…………………….

2) What are three things that could make the shields go cloudy?

    (i) …………………………………………………………………………………………………

    (ii) …………………………………………………………………………………………………

    (iii) …………………………………………………………………………………………………

3) What was the greatest honour a knight could receive? ………………………………………

4) Who did the lord of the castle leave behind to guard the castle? …………………………

5) Which of the following was the site of the battle with the giants?

    (a) A dark hollow in the forest

    (b) An island in the middle of a swift-flowing stream

    (c) A field near a dangerous swamp

    (d) A rocky platform on the edge of a cliff

6) Was the knight who guarded the gate happy about the honour? ……………………………

7) Who came first to try to get the knight to abandon his post?

    (a) A giant in disguise as a little old man trying to get into the castle

    (b) A beggar woman who called the knight a coward

    (c) A fellow knight who had been wounded and left the battle

8) Who came second to try to get the knight to abandon his post?

    (a) A giant in disguise as a little old man trying to get into the castle

    (b) A beggar woman who called the knight a coward

    (c) A fellow knight who had been wounded and left the battle

9) Who came third to try to get the knight to abandon his post?
- (a) A giant in disguise as a little old man trying to get into the castle
- (b) A beggar woman who called the knight a coward
- (c) A fellow knight who had been wounded and left the battle

10) What did the little old man try to give the knight to tempt him to leave his post?
....

11) What did the knight shout when he realised he was about to give in to temptation?
....

12) Why do you think the battle at the gate was harder than the battle with the giants?

....

13) The battle inside yourself is sometimes the hardest battle of all to win. What sort of giants are in your life that you'd like to overcome? Are there any of these:
- (i) Anger
- (ii) Frustration
- (iii) Loneliness
- (iv) Bitterness

14) Name some other giants inside you'd like to defeat in battle:

- (i) ....
- (ii) ....

15) Name three differences between this story and *The Days are Numbered*:

- (a) ....
- (b) ....
- (c) ....

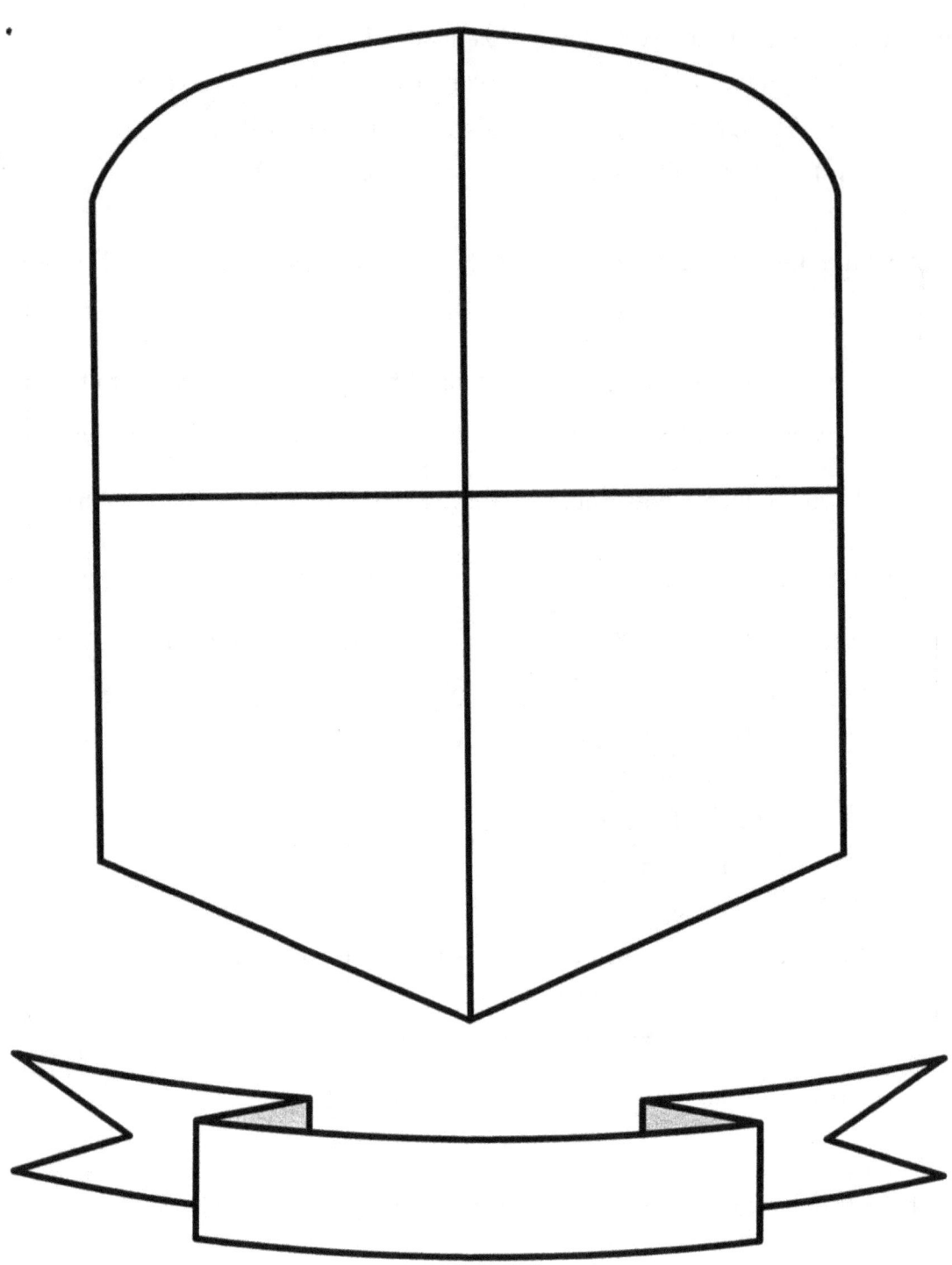

(1) **Research some clan mottos**

(2) **Make up a motto for yourself and write it on the banner**

(3) **Choose four things that could symbolise you and draw them in the quarters**

(4) **Colour**

Be Thou My Vision

Be Thou my Vision, O Lord of my heart;
Naught be all else to me, save that Thou art.
Thou my best Thought, by day or by night,
Waking or sleeping, Thy presence my light.

Be Thou my Wisdom, and Thou my true Word;
I ever with Thee and Thou with me, Lord;
Thou my great Father, I Thy true son;
Thou in me dwelling, and I with Thee one.

Be Thou my Battleshield, Sword for the fight;
Be Thou my Dignity, Thou my Delight;
Thou my soul's Shelter, Thou my high Tower:
Raise Thou me heavenward, O Power of my power.

> Alternate verse 3: Be Thou my breastplate, my sword for the fight;
> Be Thou my whole armour, be Thou my true might;
> Be Thou my soul's shelter, be Thou my strong tower:
> O raise Thou me heavenward, great Power of my power.

Riches I heed not, nor man's empty praise,
Thou mine Inheritance, now and always:
Thou and Thou only, first in my heart,
High King of heaven, my Treasure Thou art.

High King of heaven, my victory won,
May I reach heaven's joys, O bright heaven's Sun!
Heart of my own heart, whatever befall,
Still be my Vision, O Ruler of all.

(Attributed) Dallan Forgaill/ (Translated) Mary Byrne/ (Versified) Eleanor Hull

(1) This song was originally composed in the sixth century in Ireland. Even its translation is old-fashioned. What does 'Thou' mean? ....

(2) How many centuries old is Dallan Forgaill's song? ....

(3) Dallan Forgaill was blind. (Dallan is really a nickname and it means *blind*.) What is he asking in the first and last lines of the song?

....

(4) Have a go at translating the first verse into modern English:

....

....

....

....

(5) Compare the two different versions of verse 3. What is the replacement for:

    (2) Battleshield   ....

    (3) Dignity   ....

    (4) Delight   ....

    (5) The first version of verse 3 is a more accurate translation of the original language. What effect do the changes have on the meaning?

    ....

(6) This kind of song is called a 'lorica'. Find out what 'lorica' means and why were these songs called that. Write a brief explanation.

....

....

....

(7) Find the name of another lorica and its author.

    a) Name of lorica   ....

    b) Author   ....

Be Thou My Vision

Ancient Irish poem, ca. 8th cent.
Tr. by Mary E. Byrne 1905, Versified by Eleanor H. Hull 1912
Traditional Irish melody
Arr. by David Evans, 1927
Hymn Tune: SLANE

The Ballad of East and West

Rudyard Kipling (1889)

The first line of Rudyard Kipling's poem was often quoted to point out the impossibility of union between people of Western culture and those of the East. It was considered that the chasm of understanding between the two was too great to bridge. Times have changed.

Ironically, the entire poem always sent quite a different message. That East and West could come together. There is a way, as ancient as civilisation itself, for two to become one.

The ballad begins with the theft of the colonel's horse by Kamal, a Border chieftain, on the northern frontier into present-day Afghanistan. The colonel's son (who remains unnamed throughout the entire poem—a curious reversal of 'our' side being named and the 'other' side being nameless) attempts to intercept Kamal before he reaches home. Instead of turning back, as warned when he reaches the point of no return, he follows Kamal into his own lands. Death lurks on every side.

The ending of the poem is almost incomprehensibly strange in the twenty-first century. It was probably fairly odd in the nineteenth, when Kipling wrote this. However, our present loss of understanding about ancient paths of reconciliation gives it an even more abrupt, peculiar air. The poem ends with a blood covenant and all that that entails: an exchange of gifts, a mutual oath of blood brotherhood, partaking of salt and unleavened bread, the son swap, the family adoption, the appointment of an armour-bearer, the appeal to heaven.

This poem is included in these notes because the oneness between Kamal's son and the colonel's son forged by the blood covenant reflects the same kind of oneness featured at the end of *Daystar*.

> Note: This is a very difficult, old–fashioned poem and should quite possibly only be presented to those gifted and talented in English.

The Ballad of East and West

Oh, East is East, and West is West, and never the twain shall meet,
Till Earth and Sky stand presently at God's great Judgment Seat.
But there is neither East nor West, Border, nor Breed, nor Birth,
When two strong men stand face to face, though they come from the ends of the earth!

Kamal is out with twenty men to raise the Border side,
And he has lifted the Colonel's mare that is the Colonel's pride.
He has lifted her out of the stable-door between the dawn and the day,
And turned the calkins upon her feet, and ridden her far away.

Then up and spoke the Colonel's son that led a troop of the Guides:
'Is there never a man of all my men can say where Kamal hides?'
Then up and spoke Mohammed Khan, the son of the Ressaldar:
'If ye know the track of the morning-mist, ye know where his pickets are.

'At dusk he harries the Abazai—at dawn he is into Bonair,
But he must go by Fort Bukloh to his own place to fare.
So if ye gallop to Fort Bukloh as fast as a bird can fly,
By the favour of God ye may cut him off ere he win to the Tongue of Jagai.

'But if he be past the Tongue of Jagai, right swiftly turn ye then,
For the length and the breadth of that grisly plain is sown with Kamal's men.
There is rock to the left, and rock to the right, and low lean thorn between,
And ye may hear a breech-bolt snick where never a man is seen.'

The Colonel's son has taken horse, and a raw rough dun was he,
With the mouth of a bell and the heart of Hell and the head of a gallows-tree.
The Colonel's son to the fort has won, they bid him stay to eat—
Who rides at the tail of a Border thief, he sits not long at his meat.

He's up and away from Fort Bukloh as fast as he can fly,
Till he was aware of his father's mare in the gut of the Tongue of Jagai,
Till he was aware of his father's mare with Kamal upon her back,
And when he could spy the white of her eye, he made the pistol crack.

He has fired once, he has fired twice, but the whistling ball went wide.
'Ye shoot like a soldier,' Kamal said. 'Show now if you can ride!'
It's up and over the Tongue of Jagai, as blown dust-devils go,
The dun he fled like a stag of ten, but the mare like a barren doe.

The dun he leaned against the bit and slugged hi head above,
But the red mare played with the snaffle-bars, as a maiden plays with a glove.
There was rock to the right and rock to the left and low lean thorn between,
And thrice he heard a breech-bolt snick tho' never a man was seen.

They have ridden the low moon out of the sky, their hoofs drum up the dawn,
The dun he went like a wounded bull, but the mare like a new-roused fawn.
The dun he fell at a water-course—in a woeful heap fell he,
And Kamal has turned the red mare back, and pulled the rider free.

He has knocked the pistol out of his hand—small room was there to strive,
"'Twas only by favour of mine,' quoth he, 'ye rode so long alive:
There was not a rock for twenty-mile, there was not a clump of tree,
But covered a man of my own men with his rifle cocked on his knee.

'If I had raised my bridle-hand, as I have held it low,
The little jackals that flee so fast were feasting all in a row.
If I had bowed my head to my breast, as I have held it high,
The kite that whistles above us now were gorged till she could not fly.'

Lightly answered the Colonel's son: 'Do good to bird and beast,
But count who come for the broken meats before thou makest a feast.
If there should follow a thousand swords to carry my bones away,
Belike the price of a jackal's meal were more than a thief could pay.

'They will feed their horse on the standing crop, their men on the garnered grain,
The thatch of the byres will serve their fires when all the cattle are slain.
But if thou thinkest the price be fair—thy brethren wait to sup,
The hound is kin to the jackal-spawn—howl, dog, and call them up!

'And if thou thinkest the price be high—in steer and gear and stack,
Give me my father's mare again and I'll fight my own way back!'
Kamal has gripped him by the hand and set him upon his feet.
'No talk shall be of dogs,' said he, 'when wolf and grey wolf meet.

'May I eat dirt if thou hast hurt of me in deed or breath;
What dam of lances brought thee forth to jest at the dawn with Death?'
Lightly answered the Colonel's son: 'I hold by the blood of my clan:
Take up the mare for my father's gift—by God, she has carried a man!'

The red mare ran to the Colonel's son, and nuzzled against his breast;
'We be two strong men,' said Kamal then, 'but she loveth the younger best.
So she shall go with a lifter's dower, my turquoise-studded rein,
My 'broidered saddle and saddle-cloth, and silver stirrups twain.'

The Colonel's son a pistol drew, and held it muzzle-end,
'Ye have taken the one from the foe,' said he. 'Will ye take the mate from a friend?'
'A gift for a gift,' said Kamal straight; 'a limb for the risk of a limb.
Thy father has sent his son to me, I'll send my son to him!'

With that, he whistled his only son, that dropped from a mountain-crest—
He trod the ling like a buck in spring, and he looked like a lance at rest.
'Now here is thy master,' Kamal said, 'who leads a troop of the Guides,
And thou must ride at his left side as shield on shoulder rides.

'Till Death or I cut loose the tie, at camp and board and bed,
Thy life is his—thy fate it is to guard him with thy head.
So thou must eat the White Queen's meat, and all her foes are thine.
And thou must harry thy father's hold for the peace of the Border-line.

'And thou must make a trooper tough and hack thy way to power—
Belike they will raise thee to Ressalda when I am hanged in Peshawur!'
They have looked each other between the eyes and there they found no fault.
They have taken the Oath of the Brother-in-Blood on leavened bread and salt:

They have taken the Oath of the Brother-in-Blood on fire and fresh-cut sod,
On the hilt and haft of the Khyber knife, and the Wondrous Names of God.
The Colonel's son he rides the mare and Kamal's boy the dun,
And two have come back to Fort Bukloh where there went forth but one.

And when they drew to the Quarter-Guard, full twenty swords flew clear—
There was not a man but carried his feud with the blood of the mountaineer.
'Ha' done! ha' done!' said the Colonel's son. 'Put up the steel at your sides!
Last night ye had struck at a Border thief—tonight 'tis a man of the Guides!'

Oh, East is East, and West is West, and never the twain shall meet,
Till Earth and Sky stand presently at God's great Judgment Seat.
But there is neither East nor West, Border, nor Breed, nor Birth,
When two strong men stand face to face, though they come from the ends of the earth!

The land of the Border Guides

Questions:

The last seven verses of the poem describe the making of a covenant. Kamal's son and the colonel's son become blood-brothers. In doing so, they come into a closer relationship than a natural family relationship: they are 'one' with each other.

The concept seems very strange to us: Kamal's son leaves his tribe and family and nation so completely to become his blood-brother's shield-bearer that, at his father's insistence, he will now hunt his own kin.

- In a covenant ceremony, there is an exchange of gifts.
    What does the colonel's son give Kamal in exchange for the turquoise-studded rein, the embroidered saddle, saddle-cloth, and two silver stirrups? ....
    What does Kamal send to the colonel in exchange for the colonel's son? ....

- In a covenant ceremony, the family of one blood-brother becomes the family of the other.
    What does Kamal say to indicate that he expects his son to become part of the colonel's family? ....
    ....
    ....

- In a covenant ceremony, the blood-brothers eat salt to indicate the permanent nature of their vows.
    What else did Kamal's son and the colonel's son eat with the salt? ....

- In a covenant ceremony, oaths are taken.
    How did Kamal's son and the colonel's son make their vows?
    ....
    ....

- In a covenant ceremony, the blood-brothers swear to protect each other to the death.
    How is this indicated in the poem?
    ....
    ....
    ....
    ....

- In a covenant ceremony, the blood-brothers swear to protect each other's families in the event of the death of one of them.
    What is unusual about this blood-brotherhood in this regard?
    ....
    ....
    ....
    ....

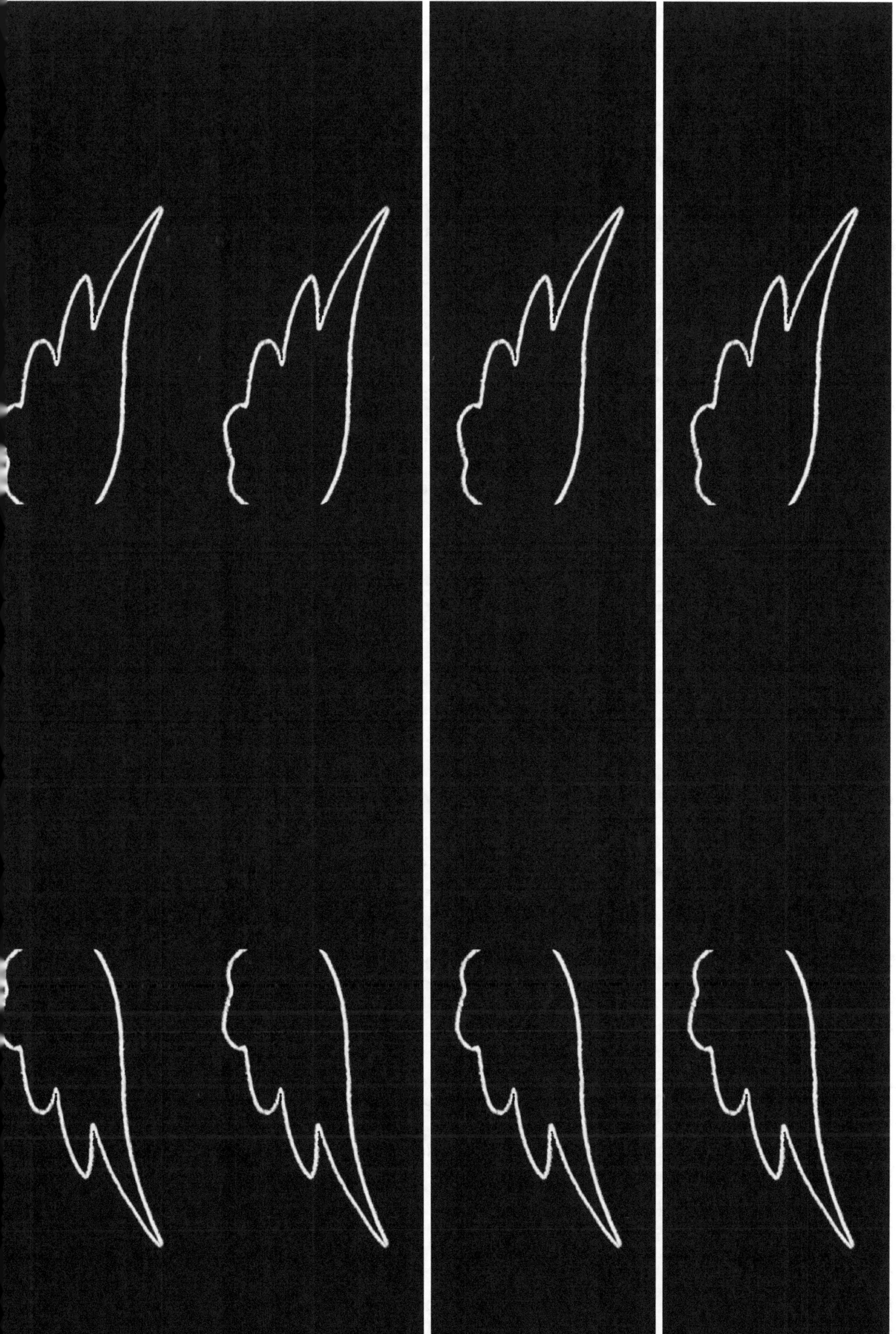

The Messenger Shoes of Peace

Make your own peace shoes just like the collar around Hector's ankles!

- Colour in the shoe collars, if desired.
- Cut with craft knife or scissors only along the marked wing line. Curl ends slightly.
- Put around ankles and check size.
- If the collars are too large, add pleats in centre.
- Place around ankles and stick together with adhesive tape.

T*H*E* B*EL*T* OF* V*ER*AC*I*T*Y*

Make your own belt or bracelet just like that of
Ginevra-'ayelet-hashachar, the fawn of dawn.

You will need:

- 3 different thin coloured ribbons (or crepe ribbons) at least 3 times the length around the waist of the person the belt is to fit
- Fabric pen
- Buckle
- Beads, tassels, studs, buttons (optional)

- Choose three different coloured ribbons (for long-lasting belt) or bands of crepe paper (for temporary belt). White, gold and silver are a good combination but any colours are suitable. The ribbons should each be three to four times the circumference of your waist
- Choose one or more of the following sayings about veracity (truth) to write on one of the ribbons:

"If you tell the truth, you don't have to remember anything." Mark Twain

"Rather than love, than money, than fame, give me truth." Henry David Thoreau

"The truth is not always beautiful, nor beautiful words the truth." Lao Tzu

"Truth never damages a cause that is just." Mahatma Gandhi

"Time is precious, but truth is more precious than time." Benjamin Disraeli

"The ideals which have always shone before me and filled me with joy are goodness, beauty, and truth." Albert Einstein

"There is no greatness where there is not simplicity, goodness, and truth." Leo Tolstoy

"Then you will know the truth and the truth will set you free." Jesus

- Fold each ribbon in half and make a slip knot on a buckle. Plait the three ribbons together loosely so the quotes can mostly be seen. Beads, buttons or tassels may be threaded onto either of the two ribbons which have not been written on. When the belt reaches the right size, knot the end tightly and cut off.

- Wear!

- Alternatively, you can make this as a bracelet. In that case, you do not need a buckle, but you might want to use flat coloured elastic as one of your 'ribbons'.

Scented Rocks

Ingredients and Utensils:

- ½ cup flour
- ½ cup salt
- ¼ tsp lavender oil
- ⅔ cup boiling water
- red and blue food colouring
- bowl, spoon, gloves

Method:

1. Mix the flour and salt together in a bowl.
2. Stir in the boiling water and lavender oil.
3. Separate the mixture into balls that are the desired size of the individual rocks.
4. Mix the 2 drops of blue with one drop of red colouring.
5. Add food colouring mixture drop by drop to each rock, swirling until your desired colour is achieved.
6. Shape the balls and allow them to dry.
7. Place them in a shallow dish or bowl for a fragrant decoration.

Tips:

1. Check the warning on the essential oil chosen. Some are poisonous, if swallowed.
2. Use different combinations of essential oils and food colouring. For example, rose geranium oil and red colouring; peppermint mix with green colouring; petitgrain and spearmint with blue colouring; vanilla oil with yellow colouring.
3. Substitute a small quantity of your favourite perfume for the essential oil.
4. Gloves are recommended, as essential oils and fragrances may be irritating to the skin.

Wrinkled Geography

Requirements:

- An old blanket or tablecloth as a painting backdrop
- A large wooden curtain ring
- Needle and thread, glue
- Acrylic paint
- Cardboard egg cartons, cardboard cylinders
- Green tissue paper, white cotton balls
- Small pebbles

To create the geography of Auberon, use the map overleaf as a guide.

(1) Attach the large wooden curtain ring to one corner with needle and thread.

(2) Then paint the rivers blue, paint the egg cartons brown and top them with cotton wool snow to create mountains.

(3) Use the tissue paper to represent swampland. Create a castle in the middle using the cardboard cylinders to create towers.

(4) Use the pebbles to show the avalanches on the Hawfell.

(5) Be creative!

(6) Once the paint and glue is dry, begin to pull a small section of the blanket through the curtain ring a couple of centimetres each day. Don't pull it all at once!

Madmerry's Potions 1

Merry's Very Berry Wash

For relaxing as a bubble bath or body wash

- ½ cup unscented shampoo or mild baby shampoo
- ¾ cup water
- ½ teaspoon table salt
- 15 drops strawberry oil
- spoon
- bowl
- decorative bottle
- label or tag

Directions:

Pour shampoo into a bowl and add water. Stir very gently until well mixed. Add salt and continue to stir while the mixture thickens. Add berry fragrance and stir once more. Carefully pour into decorative bottle. Place sticky label on bottle or tie a gift tag around the top.

Madmerry's Potions 2

Merry's Soothing Bath Soak

For relaxing as a bubble bath

- 1 cup sweet almond oil
- ½ cup honey
- ½ cup unscented liquid soap
- 1 tablespoon vanilla extract
- spoon
- bowl
- decorative bottle
- label or tag

Directions:

Pour the oil into a bowl. Stir in the other ingredients very gently until well blended. Pour into a clean bottle with a tight lid. Place sticky label on bottle or tie a gift tag around the top. *Shake gently before using.*

Seven Spiritual Sevens

Make a list of the following sevens:

- 7 commandments which include 'not'
  _____
  _____
  _____
  _____
  _____
  _____
  _____

- 7 parables of Matthew 13
  _____
  _____
  _____
  _____
  _____
  _____
  _____

- 7 signs or miracles of Jesus mentioned in John's gospel
  _____
  _____
  _____
  _____
  _____
  _____
  _____

- 7 ways Jesus claimed to be God using 'I am' in John's gospel
  _____
  _____
  _____
  _____
  _____
  _____
  _____

- 7 spiritual gifts mentioned in Romans 12
  _____
  _____
  _____
  _____
  _____
  _____
  _____

- 7 characteristics of wisdom in James 3
  _____
  _____
  _____
  _____
  _____
  _____
  _____

- 7 appearances of angels during Jesus' life on earth mentioned in all the gospels
  _____
  _____
  _____
  _____
  _____
  _____
  _____

Seven Sevenly Wonders

Make a list of the following sevens:

- 7 colours of the rainbow

- 7 continents

- 7 notes of the musical scale

- 7 oceans

- 7 wonders of the ancient world

- 7 deadly sins

Which of these wonders is accidentally mentioned by the two dwarves who are carrying Ansey up the ice stairway inside the englacial stream?

- 7 'classical' planets

Answers

Wonderword 1

Z

Cloze 1

horn, Rigel, tail, wind, Mistmurk, the Flair, folding, magic, far, earthquake, not

Identify the Character

Elsa

Wonderword 3

The leftover letter is B

Characters in B[1]

In many cases the answer depends on the viewpoint. Therefore so long as a student can justify their answer, it should be accepted.

Speed Racers

(1) 8.69 m/s; Elsa is slower than both Usain Bolt and Michael Johnson

(2) 9.98 m/s; Goliath is faster than Michael Johnson but slower than Usain Bolt

(3) 150.3 seconds or 2 minutes 30.3 seconds

(4) 6.67 m/s; Fern is much slower than Elsa and Goliath

(5) 626.4 m

(6) 37584 m or 37.584 km

Order the Events 1

4, 5, 6, 8, 10, 3, 1, 9, 2, 7

True or False? 1

F, F, T, F, F, T, F, T

Cloze 2

day, race, 1500, Green, a point, Elsa, whistle, birthday, Goliath, blows, giants, Uller, Who Guards the Gate, Ashe, Elsa, run off the track and away from the school.

Characters in C¹

In many cases the answer depends on the viewpoint. Therefore so long as a student can justify their answer, it should be accepted.

Choosing Names 2: *Star Names*

Research time:

Explain what a constellation is:

A constellation is a collection of stars which ancient peoples grouped together and thought of as representing mythological

Find the common names of three other stars in Orion:

Any of the following: Betelgeuse, Bellatrix, Alnilam, Alnitak, Saiph or Meissa

Write down the proper scientific names of the three you have chosen:

In respective order: alpha Orion, gamma Orion, epsilon Orion, zeta Orion, kappa Orion and lambda Orion

Find a picture of the Horsehead Nebula and explain what a nebula is:

A nebula is a gas cloud in space.

Find (or draw) a picture of the constellation Orion and mark the following on it: Rigel, Mintaka, Horsehead Nebula, Great Orion Nebula, Orion's Belt, Orion's Sword.

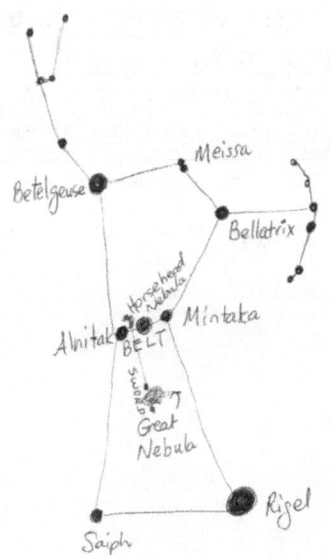

Wonderword 4

The completed title forms the word: *knighthood*

Identify the Character

Barbizca. She is both the only woman in the list and the only character described as having her hair coiled around her ears. Other justifications of the choice may be given.

Which of the pictures is a silhouette?

The third.

Cloze 3

bubble, Tree, owl, Hector, Ginevra, fawn, prince, world, destiny, eyes, dimensions, Helper, sunglasses

Assonances

Other rhymes may be given; these are samples. Check www.**rhymezone**.com

gorse, morse	Horse	→	a four-legged animal used for riding
coarse, sauce	Hoarse	→	harsh or husky sound in the throat
boars, roars	Oars	→	paddles using in the rowing of a boat
gauze, laws	Hawse	→	part of a ship's bow with openings for cables
jaws, flaws	Awes	→	causes wonder and amazement

Windows

(1) The **oriel** window is (A)

(2) Ansey

Wonderword 5

Princes

Alluring Alliteration Always Appeals

Alliteration is the use of repeated sounds in words to create a poetic style.

Order the Events 2

3, 8, 6, 10, 7, 2, 5, 4, 9, 1

True or False?

T, F, T, T, F, F, F, F, T

Wonderword 6

3 letters are left over. K O R. They stand for Knights of Renown.

Dwarf Names

All dwarf names end with the suffix '-le'. Any words ending with '-le' are suitable. All other names are giant names.

Endorsements

capable, notable, sensible, suitable, terrible

Visual Comprehension

unsheathed, unadorned, no, unblemished

Wonderword 7

none

Order the Events 3

1, 11, 8, 5, 3, 10, 7, 13, 9, 4, 2, 12, 6, 14, 15

    (1) Mistmurk
    (2) Raven
    (3) Munin and Huginn

Wonderword 8

Creature

Wonderword 9

Frost giant

Birdbrains

Pictures in order are: raven, finch, owl

Vocabulary in Chapter D²

Citadel

Order the Events 4

1, 5, 20, 7, 2, 9, 3, 6, 4, 10, 12, 8, 11, 14, 13, 19, 17, 15, 16, 18

Assonance

lattice, letters, lettuce

Scroll

The missing words are: Days, Power, unchancy, Daystar's, is, King, Guards, Gate

Choosing Names 5

Ancelin	Meaning: Servant or little god*	Language: French
Boudicca	Meaning: Victory	Language: Ancient Briton
Cindurrah	Meaning: Star Shepherd	Language: Invented
Dallan	Meaning: Blind	Language: Old Irish
Ector	Meaning: Hold Fast	Language: Greek
Fern	Meaning: Plant	Language: English
Ginevra	Meaning: Fair, white & smooth	Language: Italian

*Originally a boy's name (a variation of Lancelot), it is now commonly used also for girls.

Who's Who in Auberon and Beyond

(1) Who is the king of Auberon?
(a) Mauritz

(2) Who is the king of Fyrzentsou
(b) Rogin

(3) Who is the captain of the King's Shield?
(c) Gratian

(4) Who is the queen of Auberon?
(d) Barbizca

(5) What is Mintaka?
(d) A horse

(6) What is Rigel?
(d) A horse

(7) What is Harrowfell?
(a) A cliff

(8) What is Vircontium?
(d) A country

(9) What is Auberon?
(b) A castle

(10) Who is Tybold?
(b) Ansey's step-brother

Choosing Names 6

Seven names of seven letters.

Internet research

- Arousyag – Armenian for 'morning star'
- Ayelet – Hebrew for 'morning star'
- Bellatrix – means 'female warrior', not 'morning star'
- Danika – Slavic for 'morning star'
- Éarendel – Old English for 'morning star'
- Fetuao – Pacific Islander for 'morning star'
- Gwendydd – Old Welsh for 'morning star' (used for both girls and boys)
- Heylel – Hebrew for 'to shine'; often mistakenly translated 'morning star'
- Jesus — does not mean 'morning star' but 'God saves'. One of the titles of Jesus Christ is the Bright and Morning Star

- Keiyona – Hindu name for 'morning star'
- Kōpū – Maori name for 'morning star'
- Lucifer – name means 'light bearer'; often mistakenly used for the 'morning star'
- Sitara – Sanskrit name for 'morning star'
- Tariq – Arabic name for 'morning star'
- Zornitsa – Bulgarian name for 'morning star'

Water inside Water

Currents are flows of water inside water. The Gulf Stream, for example, is a flow of warm water inside the colder water of the Atlantic Ocean.

Naming Days 1

1. Seventh Day

2. Happy

3. It's the seventh in the order of the poem.

4. Saturday

5.

Sunday's Child	Ansey
Monday's Child	Fern
Tuesday's Child	Hector
Wednesday's Child	Fern
Thursday's Child	Ginevra
Friday's Child	Madmerry
Saturday's Child	Dallan

6. Not really

Book Link

(a) Solveigra
(b) The White Mother
(c) Immortality
(d) Youth
(e) A desire for beauty
(f) Stairway

Naming Days 2

Sunday is named after	The sun
Monday is named after	The moon
Tuesday is named after	Tiw
Wednesday is named after	Woden
Thursday is named after	Thor
Friday is named after	Freyja
Saturday is named after	Saturn

Research:

English	French	German
Sunday	Dimanche	Sonntag
Monday	Lundi	Montag
Tuesday	Mardi	Dienstag
Wednesday	Mercredi	Mittwoch
Thursday	Jeudi	Donnerstag
Friday	Vendredi	Freitag
Saturday	Samedi	Samstag

Mercury, Venus, Mars, Jupiter and Saturn should be circled.

Cirques

The Bowl of the Field of Stars

Language	Word for *bowl in the landscape*	Meaning
Latin	Cirque	Arena
Scots	Corrie	Pot *or* Cauldron

| Welsh | Cwm | Valley |
| Hebrew | Makhtesh | Mortar Grinder |

The names of the four cirques in Australia are: Blue Lake, Cootapatamba, Albina, and Club

Grounded!

Stalactite	A rock formation that rises from the floor of a cave and is composed of deposits from ceiling drippings
Stalagmite	A rock formation that hangs from the ceiling of caves
Englacial Stream	A flow of meltwater inside a glacier
Rose Quartz	A semi-precious gemstone like glass with a pale pink to rosy red colouring
Amethyst	A form of quartz that has a purplish or lilac colouring
Crevasse	A deep crack in an ice sheet or glacier
Crevice	A deep crack in rock
Avalanche	Snowslide or snowslip; a rapid fall of snow down a slope
Cirque	A bowl-shaped valley at the head of a glacier
Glacier	A large body of dense ice moving extremely slowly downhill under its own weight

Wonderword 10

The title is **In the Tunnel!**

Nicknames

1. Ancelin — real name
2. Ansey — nickname for Ancelin Bedwyr Cai
3. Boody — nickname for Boudicca's Chariot
4. Boudicca's Chariot — real name
5. Boy Wonder — nickname for Dallan
6. Cindurrah — real name
7. Dallan — pseudonym for Emyr
8. Ector — real name
9. Emyr — real name
10. Fern — real name
11. Ginevra — real name
12. Hector — pseudonym for Ector
13. Madmerry — pseudonym for Cindurrah
14. Merry — nickname for Madmerry

What is a nickname? A shortened substitute for the proper name of a person.

Wonderword 11
Folk of Ysgarde

Sun, Moon & Stars
The stars are like flowers.

Order the Events 5
1, 8, 17, 11, 15, 2, 4, 12, 3, 16, 14, 6, 5, 9, 7, 10, 13, 18

Wonderword 12

- 60 minutes = 1 minute
- 7 days = 1 week
- 4 weeks = 1 month
- 52 weeks = 1 year
- 1 fortnight = 2 weeks
- 10 years = 1 decade
- 366 days = 1 leap year
- 60 seconds = one minute

Playing with Ones (1)

$1 + 1 = 2$
$1 + 1 + 1 = 3$
$1 + 1 + 1 + 1 = 4$
$1 + 1 + 1 + 1 + 1 = 5$
$1 + 1 + 1 + 1 + 1 + 1 = 6$
$1 + 1 + 1 + 1 + 1 + 1 + 1 = 7$

We learn to count so we don't have to keep on adding up **ones**.

1 + 1 = 2 lots of ones
1 + 1 + 1 = 3 lots of ones
1 + 1 + 1 + 1 = 4 lots of ones
1 + 1 + 1 + 1 + 1 = 5 lots of ones

1 + 1 + 1 + 1 + 1 + 1 = 6 lots of ones
1 + 1 + 1 + 1 + 1 + 1 + 1 = 7 lots of ones

1 + 1 = 2 × 1
1 + 1 + 1 = 3 × 1
1 + 1 + 1 + 1 = 4 × 1
1 + 1 + 1 + 1 + 1 = 5 × 1
1 + 1 + 1 + 1 + 1 + 1 = 6 × 1
1 + 1 + 1 + 1 + 1 + 1 + 1 = 7 × 1
11 + 11 + 11 + 11 + 11 + 11 + 11 + 11 + 11 + 11 + 11 = 11 × 11 = 121
111 + 111 + 111 + 111 + 111 + 111 + 111 + 111 + 111 + 111 + 111 + 111 + 111 +
111 + 111 + 111 + 111 + 111 + 111 + 111 + 111 + 111 + 111 + 111 + 111 + 111 +
111 + 111 + 111 + 111 + 111 + 111 + 111 + 111 + 111 + 111 + 111 + 111 + 111 +
111 + 111 + 111 + 111 + 111 + 111 + 111 + 111 + 111 + 111 + 111 + 111 + 111 +
111 + 111 + 111 + 111 + 111 + 111 + 111 + 111 + 111 + 111 + 111 + 111 + 111 +
111 + 111 + 111 + 111 + 111 + 111 + 111 + 111 + 111 + 111 + 111 + 111 + 111 +
111 + 111 + 111 + 111 + 111 + 111 + 111 + 111 + 111 + 111 + 111 + 111 + 111 +
111 + 111 + 111 + 111 + 111 + 111 + 111 + 111 + 111 + 111 + 111 + 111 + 111 +
111 + 111 + 111 + 111 + 111 + 111 + 111 = 111 × 111 = 12321

How many lots of 11 would you have to add up if you wanted the answer to equal the same as 11 × 7? **seven**

How many lots of 11 would you have to add up if you wanted the answer to equal the same as 11 × 17? **seventeen**

How many lots of 11 would you have to add up if you wanted the answer to equal the same as 11 × 111? **one hundred and eleven**

How many lots of 111 would you have to add up if you wanted the answer to equal the same as 111 × 7? **seven**

How many lots of 111 would you have to add up if you wanted the answer to equal the same as 111 × 17? **seventeen**

How many lots of 111 would you have to add up if you wanted the answer to equal the same as 111 × 1111? **one thousand one hundred and eleven**

How many lots of 1111 would you have to add up if you wanted the answer to equal the same as 1111 × 1111? **one thousand one hundred and eleven**

How many lots of 11111 would you have to add up if you wanted the answer to equal the same as 1111 × 11111? **one thousand one hundred and eleven**

How many lots of 1111111 would you have to add up if you wanted the answer to equal the same as 1111111111 × 1111111? **one billion, one hundred and eleven million, one hundred and eleven thousand, one hundred and eleven**

Playing with Ones (2)

1 × 9 + 2 = 11
12 × 9 + 3 = 111
123 × 9 + 4 = 1111
1234 × 9 + 5 = 11111
12345 × 9 + 6 = 111111

123456 × 9 + 7 = 1111111
1234567 × 9 + 8 = 11111111
12345678 × 9 + 9 = 111111111

Does the pattern keep working for 123456789 × 9 + 10? Yes. 1111111111
However it does not work for 12345678910 × 9 + 11 or subsequent numbers.

Choosing **Names** 9: *AKA ~ Also Known As*

Ansey	aka	Ancelin Bedwyr Cai		
Boody	aka	Boudicca's Chariot		
Madmerry	aka	Cindurrah	aka	Merry
Dallan	aka	Boy Wonder	aka	Emyr
Hector	aka	Ector		
Ginevra	aka	Ginevra-'ayelet-hashachar		
Candle	aka	Lord of the Nardelf		
Gratian	aka	Lord Commander of Ysgarde		
Solveigra	aka	Wreathwatch Woman		
Uller	aka	Princekiller	aka	Xerxes Xenophon
Quystein	aka	The Q		
The Song	aka	Ruēl	aka	The Ancient of Days

Playing with Ones (3)

1 × 1 = 1
11 × 11 = 121
111 × 111 = 12321
1111 × 1111 = 1234321
11111 × 11111 = 123454321
111111 × 111111 = 12345654321
1111111 × 1111111 = 1234567654321
11111111 × 11111111 = 123456787654321
111111111 × 111111111 = 12345678987654321
Does the pattern still hold for 1111111111 × 1111111111?
No, the pattern breaks down. 1111111111 × 1111111111 = 1234567900987654321
There is an 8 missing.

Playing with Ones (4)

1 × 8 + 1 = 9
12 × 8 + 2 = 98
123 × 8 + 3 = 987
1234 × 8 + 4 = 9876
12345 × 8 + 5 = 98765
123456 × 8 + 6 = 987654
1234567 × 8 + 7 = 9876543
12345678 × 8 + 8 = 98765432

123456789 × 8 +9 = 987654321

Does the pattern still work for 1234567890 × 8 +10? No, it is 9876543130

Playing with Ones (5)

(1) In what place is the one in 10000 standing? Ten thousands
(2) In what place is the one in 100 standing? Hundreds
(3) In what place is the one in 1000000 standing? Millions
(4) In what place is the one in 10 standing? Tens
(5) In what place is the 3 in 300 standing? Hundreds
(6) In what place is the 5 in 5000 standing? Thousands

Playing with Ones (6)

10 + 1 = 11
100 + 1 = 101
1000 + 1 = 1001
10000 + 1 = 10001

100 + 10 = 110
1000 + 100 = 1100
10000 + 1000 = 11000
100000 + 10000 = 110000

100 + 10 + 1 = 111
1000 + 100 + 10 = 1110
10000 + 1000 + 100 = 11100
100000 + 10000 + 1000 = 111000

1000 + 100 + 10 + 1 = 1111
10000 + 1000 + 100 + 10 = 11110
100000 + 10000 + 1000 + 100 = 111100

10000 + 1000 + 100 + 10 + 1 = 11111
100000 + 10000 + 1000 + 100 + 10 = 111110
100000 + 10000 + 1000 + 100 + 10 + 1 = 111111

Playing with Ones (7)

Powers

$1 \times 1 = 1$ to the power 2 = 1^2 = 1
$1 \times 1 \times 1 = 1$ to the power 3 = 1^3 = 1
$1 \times 1 \times 1 \times 1 = 1$ to the power 4 = 1^4 = 1
$1 \times 1 \times 1 \times 1 \times 1 = 1$ to the power 5 = 1^5 = 1
$1 \times 1 \times 1 \times 1 \times 1 \times 1 = 1$ to the power 6 = 1^6 = 1

$1 \times 1 \times 1 \times 1 \times 1 \times 1 \times 1 = 1$ to the power 7 = 1^7 = 1
$1 \times 1 \times 1 \times 1 \times 1 \times 1 \times 1 \times 1 = 1$ to the power 8 = 1^8 = 1
$1 \times 1 \times 1 \times 1 \times 1 \times 1 \times 1 \times 1 \times 1 = 1$ to the power 9 = 1^9 = 1
$1 \times 1 \times 1 \times 1 \times 1 \times 1 \times 1 \times 1 \times 1 \times 1 = 1$ to the power 10 = 1^{10} = 1
$1 \times 1 \times 1 \times 1 \times 1 \times 1 \times 1 \times 1 \times 1 \times 1 \times 1 = 1$ to the power 11 = 1^{11} = 1
$11 \times 11 = 11$ to the power 2 = 11^2 = 121
$11 \times 11 \times 11 = 11$ to the power 3 = 11^3 = 1331
$11 \times 11 \times 11 \times 11 = 11$ to the power 4 = 11^4 = 14641

How would you write:
11^1 = 11
11^0 = 1

Gemstones

1. Ruby — bright red
2. Emerald — bright green
3. Violane — purple
4. Argyll diamond — orangish yellow
5. Peridot — pale green
6. Jet — black
7. Garnet — crimson red
8. Topaz — yellow, brown or blue
9. Citrine — yellowish green
10. Carnelian — deep red
11. Amber — brown or yellow
12. Jade — green
13. Chyrsoprase — creamy green
14. Amethyst — purple
15. rose quartz — pink

Inventing Words

There are many words Shakespeare invented; these are some but there are many others.

1. Addiction
2. Arch-villain
3. Assassination
4. Bedazzled
5. Belongings
6. Cold-blooded
7. Dishearten
8. Eventful
9. Eyeball
10. Fashionable
11. Half-blooded/hot-blooded

12. Inaudible
13. Ladybird
14. Manager
15. Multitudinous
16. New-fangled
17. Pageantry
18. Scuffle
19. Swagger
20. Uncomfortable

Wonderword 13

- Speaking Sword
- Messenger Shoes
- Belt of Veracity
- Mailcoat of Justice
- Helmet of Providence
- Daystar Shield
- grace cloaks
- The Song

The missing colour is purple or violet.

Order the Events 6

18, 9, 3, 13, 5, 2, 6, 8, 1, 20, 11, 19, 7, 4, 12, 16, 15, 17, 14, 10

Order the Events 7

1, 15, 16, 6, 4, 5, 7, 2, 12, 13, 8, 11, 9, 14, 10, 3, 17

Music of the Grace Cloaks

(1) What is another name for a minim? Half note

(2) What is another name for a whole note? Semi-breve

(3) What is another name for a quarter note? Crochet

(4) What is another name for a quaver? Eighth note

(5) What is another name for a semi-breve? Whole note

(6) What is another name for a semi-quaver? Sixteenth note

(7) What is another name for a whole rest? Semibreve rest

(8) What is another name for a demi-semi-quaver? Thirty-second note

(9) What is another name for a half note? Minim

(10) What is another name for a sixteenth note? Semi-quaver

(11) What is another name for a thirty-secondth note? Demi-semi-quaver

(12) What is another name for an eighth note? Quaver

(13) What is another name for a crotchet? Quarter Note

(14) What is another name for a semibreve rest? Whole rest

(15) Find out what a treble clef is and draw one here. 𝄞

(16) Draw a minim. 𝅗𝅥

(17) Draw a crotchet. ♩

(18) Draw a semibreve. 𝅝

(19) Draw a semibreve rest. ▬

(20) Draw a quaver. ♪

(21) Draw a semi-quaver. 𝅘𝅥𝅯

(22) Draw a demi-semi-quaver. 𝅘𝅥𝅰

(23) Draw a whole note. 𝅝

(24) Draw a half note. 𝅗𝅥

(25) Draw a quarter note. ♩

(26) Is a quarter note the same as a quaver? No, a quarter note is a crochet.

(27) Find out what an octave is and write an explanation here: a series of eight notes occupying the interval between (and including) the first and the last note, the first having twice or half the frequency of vibration of the last.

(28) Mark in the musical note hummed by the red grace cloak as a red crotchet.

A red ♩ should be marked in the space between the third and fourth lines (counting down).

(29) Mark in the musical note hummed by the yellow grace cloak as a yellow quaver.

A yellow 𝅘𝅥𝅮 should be between the second and third lines (counting down).

(30) Mark in the musical note hummed by the indigo grace cloak as a midnight blue minim.

A blue 𝅗𝅥 should be on the top line.

(31) Mark in the musical note hummed by the orange grace cloak as an orange semi-quaver.

An orange 𝅘𝅥𝅯 should be on the fourth line (counting down).

(32) Mark in the musical note hummed by the purple grace cloak as a purple semibreve rest.

A purple 𝄻 should be just above the top line.

(33) Mark in the musical note hummed by the green grace cloak as a green semi-breve.

A green 𝅝 should be on the second line from the top.

(34) Mark in the musical note hummed by the blue grace cloak as a blue semi-quaver.

A blue 𝅘𝅥𝅯 should be between the top line and the next line down.

(35) Mark in the musical note hummed by Ansey's grace cloak as a quaver. Choose the appropriate colour to match the cloak.

A red 𝅘𝅥𝅮 between the third and fourth lines (counting down).

(36) Mark in the musical note hummed by Fern's grace cloak as a quaver. Choose the appropriate colour to match the cloak.

An orange 𝅘𝅥𝅮 on the fourth line (counting down).

(37) Mark in the musical note hummed by Hector's grace cloak as a quaver. Choose the appropriate colour to match the cloak.

A blue 𝅘𝅥𝅮 between the top line and the next line down

(38) Mark in the musical note hummed by Boody's grace cloak as a quaver. Choose the appropriate colour to match the cloak.

A yellow 𝅘𝅥𝅮 between the second and third lines (counting down).

(39) Mark in the musical note hummed by Emyr's grace cloak as a quaver. Choose the appropriate colour to match the cloak.

A purple ♪ just above the top line.

(40) Mark in the musical note hummed by Birds and Fishes grace cloak as a quaver. Choose the appropriate colour to match the cloak.

A blue ♪ between the top line and the next line down

(41) Mark in the musical note hummed by Sea and Sky grace cloak as a quaver. Choose the appropriate colour to match the cloak.

An orange ♪ on the fourth line (counting down).

Applying Logic

Colour	Character
RED	Ansey
ORANGE	Fern
YELLOW	Boody
GREEN	Ginevra
BLUE	Hector
INDIGO	Madmerry
VIOLET	Emyr

Gemstones

Colour	Gemstones	Similar Colour
RED	carnelian, garnet, ruby	sardonyx
ORANGE	amber, topaz, tiger-eye	fire opal, sunstone
YELLOW	argyll diamond, lemon chrysoprase	cymophane
GREEN	citrine, emerald, jade, peridot	greenstone, jadeite
BLUE	aquamarine, blue topaz, lapis lazuli, sapphire	turquoise
INDIGO	Jet	iolite
VIOLET	violane, amethyst	kunzite, sugilite

See ~ http://kamayojewelry.com/category/gemstone-colors/

Naming Days 3 ~ A Surfeit of Princes

What does *surfeit* mean? Too many or too much

The four princes are: Ansey, Emyr, Gratian, Tybold

Research:

What is the correct name for a group or collection of:

	Group name
Princes	State
Finches	Charm
Ravens	Unkindness
Knights	Banner
Giants	Percussion
Boys	Blush
Girls	Bevy
Fish	School

Threes

White Three at the White Tree: Boody; Hector; Ginevra
Kinds of birds: owls; finches; ravens
Species: humans; giants; dwarves
Kings: Rogin; Maurtz; Candle

CONFIDENTIAL!

Candle	Knows where the secret entrance to the tunnel under the Wreathwatch Mountains is
Gratian	Is not a simple captain but the Commander of the Knights of Renown
Dallan	Is not a simple sheep-herder but the rightful king of Fyrzentsou
Madmerry	Is hiding one of the Seven Powers and wearing it under a decorated headpiece
Hector	Is hiding one of the Seven Powers and wearing it around his ankles
Uller	Has secretly collected seven grace cloaks and decides to risk all when he realises who The Days are
Ansey	Has secretly practised swordplay when he was loaned a sword by an injured squire
Maurtz	Knows the landscape is folding and wrinkling but is trying to hide it by using marble rollers to smooth out the lawns

Naming Days 4: Titles

Anointed High **King**, Lord of The **Nardelf**, Enthroned **Serenity** on the Rock of **Time**, Master of The Deeping Ways, Warden of the Scimitar **Mountains**, Well-builder of the **Stars**, Son of **Earth** and Child of **Ancient** Dream

King of the **Frost** Giants, Ruler of the **Jotun** Alliance

Chief Prince of the **High** Command of **Ysgarde**

'The White Three from the White Tree' are Hector, Boody and Ginevra

Uller calls Madmerry and Dallan 'The Masked Duo'.

Fern becomes the 'Perfect Helper'.

Ansey is 'The King Who Guards the Gate'.

The 'Days' are Ansey, Fern, Emyr (Dallan), Hector, Madmerry, Boody, Ginevra.

A, B, C, D, E, F and G make up the notes hummed by the grace cloaks.

Collective Nouns

Single element	Group name
Day	Week
Owl	Parliament
Fox	Skulk
Deer	Herd
Finch	Charm
Raven	Storytelling
Soldier	Platoon

2. The wrong answers are:

   (a) a fury of foxes
   (b) a darling of deer
   (c) a croak of ravens
   (d) a saddle of horses
   (e) a leep of leopards, a lope of leopards
   (f) a frying of fish
   (g) a shield of knights
   (h) a spinney of trees, a season of trees
   (i) a squid of soldiers
   (j) a band of asteroids, a twinkle of asteroids

3. Match the following:

Single element	Group name
Zebra	Zeal
Chihuahua	Yap
Hedgehog	Prickle
Cat	Kendle
Jellyfish	Fluther
Duck	Badelynge

From http://users.tinyonline.co.uk/gswithenbank/collnoun.htm

The Armour of the Daystar

Item of Armour	Character
helmet	Madmerry
Shoes	Hector
Shield	Ansey
Mailcoat	Boody
Belt	Ginevra
Sword	Emyr/Dallan
Lance	None

Who said that?

1. The land's cursed. It's folding in on itself. **A soldier of the King's Shield**
2. A good king serves his people through his rule. **Ansey**
3. Those of us who get on with life find destiny seeking us out. We don't have to wait around for it, it's there waiting for us. **Ginevra**
4. I always was a sucker for a prince with pretty manners. **Candle**
5. Can you tell me if this is where I might find The King Who Guards The Gate? **Uller**
6. Do you want healing for your heart or your soul? **Dallan**
7. Her weakness is the desire for beauty. **Ancient of Days**
8. When the Days come, assuming their Power, then is the time unchancy late. **Uller**
9. The Fifth Dwarf Legion at your service. **Stubble**

10. Seven Days do not make One Week, they simply are weak. **Candle**

11. Uller Princekiller is my name, and royalty's passing is my game. **Uller**

12. There is nothing in the entire universe, absolutely nothing, more terrifying than a nursery bogeyman that's even partly real. **Hector**

13. Penthouse suite to your right. Have a nice day. **The lift**

14. Wobble, Nobble, Monday, Tuesday, Wednesday, Thursday, Friday, Saturday and Sunday. Here to save the day. Which is obviously a brand new day, because the rest of the week is already accounted for. **Wobble**

15. You *can't* sell human beings. It's *not right*. **Ansey**

16. Grace cloaks don't actually exist. They're just legends from the time of tribulation after the Englobing. **Tobias**

17. Hey look, guys, I'm a *flying fox*! **Hector**

18. Douse the lights, douse the lights. **Huginn**

19. Without the single heartbeat within this armour, without the single song in all its harmonic splendour shaping its form, this is a pile of useless junk. **Ginevra**

20. What's the chance of getting a mobile phone of my own? I realised I don't need an opposable thumb to operate one. **Hector**

Picky Pairs

The true statements are:

- Frost giants pull heat from the air; that's why it's chilly around them
- Dwarves and giants have been enemies for centuries
- Ysgarde rides on a pseudolithic cushion and only looks like it's built on rock
- The Smoke Squadron used smoke to disturb the giants and ice up the field of battle
- There is at least one woman fighter in the Knights of Renown
- Lord Quystein wanted to kill off the giants but Lord Ancelin wouldn't let him
- The Acting Commander of the Knights of Renown is Quystein
- Ansey faces three trials of his honour when he is guarding the gate

Odd One **Out**

(1) Which of the following is not human? (d) Hector

(2) Which of the following is not female? (c) Candle

(3) Which of the following is not male? (d) Barbizca

(4) Which of the following is not a prince? (d) Candle

(5) Which of the following is not one of Ansey's tutors? (a) Gratian

(6) Which of the following is not one of the White Three of the White Tree? (d) Fern McDey

(7) Which of the following is not white? (d) Madmerry

(8) Which of the following is not a dwarf? (d) Tobias

(9) Which of the following is not a kingdom? (b) The White Tree

(10) Which of the following is not royalty? (b) Fern

(11) Which of the following is not a feature of the landscape? (d) Ysgarde

(12) Which of the following do not attend Fern's school? (d) Uller

(13) Which of the following is not known to be available at the foodstalls in Auberon? (d) Hamburger

(14) Which of the following is not a bird? (d) Uller

(15) Which of the following is not a horse? (d) Huginn

(16) Which of the following do not have Flair? (d) Gratian

(17) Which of the following is not a giant? (c) Munin and (d) Huginn

(18) Which of the following is not a monster? (b) Snow leopards

(19) Which of the following is not a member of The Days? (c) Candle

(20) Which of the following is not the colour of a grace cloak? (a) Pink

(21) Which of the following is not a variety of giant? (d) Gas

(22) Which of the following is not a Knight of Renown? (d) Freutim of the Jotun Alliance

(23) Which of the following was not given by The Song to Ansey? (c) A briefcase

(24) Which of the following people did not visit Ansey while he was guarding the gate of Ysgarde? (c) Wreathwatch Woman

(25) Which of the following was not given by Candle as a gift to The Days? (d) Cellphone

(26) Which of the following is not a sign that Fyrzentsou's true king has returned? (c) Firepetals fall from the sun and (d) Jewels drop out of the sky

(27) Which of the following is not a member of the Smoke Squadron? (a) Ansey

(28) Which of the following people is not wearing a disguise of some sort? (d) Ancelin Bedwyr Cai

(29) Which of the following is not a manifestation of the Dark Sleeper? (d) Creeper

(30) Which of the following is not one of the Seven Powers? (d) Whispering Ring

The Knights of the Silver Shield COMPREHENSION

(1) They carried a long spear. They wore a helmet with a great red plume. They had a special shield.

(2) Three things that could make the shields go cloudy were:
- laziness or cowardice
- not caring what happened to travellers
- letting the giants get the upper hand

(3) What was the greatest honour a knight could receive? A gold star could appear on the silver shield.

(4) Roland

(5) (a) a dark hollow in the forest

(6) no

(7) (c) A fellow knight who had been wounded and left the battle

(8) (b) A beggar woman who called the knight a coward

(9) (a) A giant in disguise as a little old man trying to get into the castle

(10) A sword

(11) 'No!'

(12) It was a battle inside Roland's self

(15) Any three differences are an acceptable answer.

Be Thou My Vision

What does 'Thou' mean? You

How many centuries old is Dallan Forgaill's song? 15

What is Dallan Forgaill asking in the first and last lines of the song? For God to be his eyes

A possible translation into modern English is:

> *Come be my vision, o Lord of my heart,*
> *Be nothing else to me than what you are.*
> *You're my best thought, each day and each night*
> *Awake or asleep, Your presence is light.*

The replacement for:

- Battleshield is Breastplate
- Dignity is Armour
- Delight is Might

The first version of verse 3 is a more accurate translation of the original language. What effect do the changes have on the meaning? They change references to covenant into warfare words.

'Lorica' means *breastplate*. Such songs were considered to bring God's protection into a person's life.

The most famous lorica is *The Deer's Cry* (also called *St Patrick's Breastplate*) written by Patrick, the patron saint of Ireland.

Questions on The Ballad of East and West:

- In a covenant ceremony, there is an exchange of gifts.
  What does the colonel's son give Kamal in exchange for the turquoise-studded rein, the embroidered saddle, saddle-cloth, and two silver stirrups? A pistol
  What does Kamal send to the colonel in exchange for the colonel's son? His son

- In a covenant ceremony, the family of one blood-brother becomes the family of the other. What does Kamal say to indicate that he expects his son to become part of the colonel's family? '...thou must ride at his left side as shield on shoulder rides. Till Death or I cut loose the tie, at camp and board and bed, Thy life is his—thy fate it is to guard him with thy head.'

- In a covenant ceremony, the blood-brothers eat salt to indicate the permanent nature of their vows. What else did Kamal's son and the colonel's son eat with the salt? bread

- In a covenant ceremony, oaths are taken. How did Kamal's son and the colonel's son make their vows? On fire and fresh-cut sod, on the hilt and haft of the Khyber knife, and the Wondrous Names of God.

- In a covenant ceremony, the blood-brothers swear to protect each other to the death. How is this indicated in the poem? 'Ha' done! ha' done!' said the Colonel's son. 'Put up the steel at your sides! Last night ye had struck at a Border thief—tonight 'tis a man of the Guides!'

- In a covenant ceremony, the blood-brothers swear to protect each other's families in the event of the death of one of them. What is unusual about this blood-brotherhood in this regard? The father says that his son should be against his own family and tribe, in order to protect the Colonel's son.

Seven Spiritual Sevens

- 7 commandments which include 'not'

    1. You shall not make idols.
    2. You shall not dishonour the name of God.
    3. You shall not murder.
    4. You shall not commit adultery.
    5. You shall not steal.
    6. You shall not tell lies.
    7. You shall not covet.

- 7 parables of Matthew 13

    1. Parable of the Sower
    2. Parable of the Weeds
    3. Parable of the Mustard Seed
    4. Parable of the Leaven
    5. Parable of the Hidden Treasure
    6. Parable of the Pearl
    7. Parable of Drawing in the Net

- 7 signs or miracles of Jesus mentioned in John's gospel

    1. Changing water into wine
    2. Healing the royal official's son
    3. Healing the paralytic at Bethesda
    4. Feeding the 5000
    5. Jesus' walk on water
    6. Healing the man born blind
    7. Raising of Lazarus

- 7 ways Jesus claimed to be God using 'I am' in John's gospel

    1. I am the bread of life.
    2. I am the light of the world.
    3. I am the door.
    4. I am the good shepherd.
    5. I am the resurrection and the life.
    6. I am the way, the truth, and the life.
    7. I am the true vine.

- 7 spiritual gifts mentioned in Romans 12

1. Prophesying
2. Serving
3. Teaching
4. Encouraging
5. Giving
6. Leading
7. Showing Mercy

- 7 characteristics of wisdom in James 3
    1. pure
    2. peace-loving
    3. considerate
    4. submissive
    5. full of mercy and good fruit
    6. impartial
    7. sincere

- 7 appearances of angels during Jesus' life on earth mentioned in all the gospels

    1. Visited Mary to announce she was chosen – Luke 1:30-33
    2. Announced his birth to the shepherds – Luke 2:10-14
    3. Appeared to Joseph in a dream to warn of Herod's plot – Matt. 2:19, 20
    4. Ministry after Jesus' temptation – Matt. 4:11
    5. Ministry in the Garden of Gethsemane – Luke 22:43
    6. Rolled back the stone from the tomb and announced resurrection – Matt. 28:2-6
    7. Ascension of Christ – Acts 1:11

Seven Sevenly Wonders

- 7 colours of the rainbow
  Red
    1. Orange
    2. Yellow
    3. Green
    4. Blue
    5. Indigo
    6. Violet

- 7 notes of the musical scale
  A, B, C, D, E, F, G

- 7 wonders of the ancient world

    1. The Great Pyramid of Giza

2. The Colossus of Rhodes
3. The Lighthouse of Alexandria
4. The Mausoleum at Halicarnassus
5. The Temple of Artemis
6. The Statue of Zeus

Which of these wonders is accidentally mentioned by the two dwarves who are carrying Ansey up the ice stairway inside the englacial stream? The pyramid

- 7 continents
  Asia, Africa, North America, South America, Europe, Australia and Antarctica.

- 7 seas

  1. the Arctic Ocean
  2. the North Atlantic Ocean
  3. the South Atlantic Ocean
  4. the Indian Ocean
  5. the North Pacific Ocean
  6. the South Pacific Ocean
  7. the Southern (or Antarctic) Ocean

- 7 deadly sins
  1. Lust
  2. Gluttony
  3. Greed
  4. Sloth
  5. Wrath
  6. Envy
  7. Pride

- 7 Classical 'Planets'
  1. Sun
  2. Moon
  3. Mercury
  4. Venus
  5. Mars
  6. Jupiter
  7. Saturn

www.ingramcontent.com/pod-product-compliance
Lightning Source LLC
Chambersburg PA
CBHW050713090526
44587CB00019B/3363